Introduction

Since the end of the Cold War at the beginning of the 1990s, growing state and global instability, particularly in undergoverned regions of the world, has led to increasing requests from ambassadors and combatant commanders for civil affairs forces to conduct missions in support of a whole-of-government (WOG) approach aimed at improving and sustaining stability, and preventing war. In the same two decades, U.S. military forces have conducted combat operations in Afghanistan and Iraq, stability operations in Bosnia, Kosovo and Somalia, and conducted other Operation Enduring Freedom missions around the globe, all requiring a civil military operations (CMO) component. More than ninety percent of the civil affairs force structure is in the U.S. Army Reserve in support of conventional forces, with only one brigade in the active component for special operations and contingency missions. Based on increasing government emphasis on whole-of-government operations to maintain stability and protect U.S. interests, in addition to persistent counterinsurgency and foreign internal defense operations –of which civil military operations are a key component—the authorized growth in civil affairs forces will not meet the increasing demand. The purpose of this monograph is to discern an appropriate civil affairs force structure to conduct civil affairs operations in support of persistent whole-of-government stability, security, transition, and reconstruction (SSTR) efforts and support military forces in long-term full spectrum operations in Iraq, Afghanistan, the Philippines, and other undergoverned states in order to improve stability of the international state system.

Since the collapse of the Soviet Union, existential threat to the United States from state actors has diminished drastically and realist theories have given way in favor of more liberal approaches. In this era of global dominance since the end of the Cold War, the United States has adopted liberal hegemonic stability theory to guide its foreign policy.[1] While administrations may shift to more liberal or more realist application of the theory, references to American 'leadership' in the international community

---

[1] Graham Evens and Jeffrey Newnham, *Dictionary of International Relations*, (New York: Penguin Books, 1998), 220-221.

abound in the National Security, Defense and Military Strategies. As the most powerful nation-state in the world, the United States has assumed a leading role in the global community in the enforcement of international rule sets based on laws and customs with the intent of maintaining stable global security and economic systems.[2] Thomas P.M. Barnett has argued that the United States should create a system administrator, or rule set enforcement organization, separate from the military. The system administrator would apply non-military national power to encourage non-compliant states to conform to accepted international norms. The military would be used as a last resort.[3] This line of argument is reflective of liberalism, which prefers soft power over hard power. Joseph Nye asserts that while budgeting for instruments of soft power declined after the Cold War, the need for soft power was growing. It was not until the events of September 2001 did Americans realize our overreliance on hard power.[4]

Christopher Layne argues that many U.S. policymakers foolhardily pursue hegemonic exceptionalism, believing that the benevolent American version will avoid the historical record of hegemonic defeat.[5] Exceptionalism – also referred to as American messianism or idealism – is the belief that the United States is 'set apart' from the rest of the world by God as an example of democracy, free market economy, and liberty. Adherents to exceptionalism believe the United States has a 'mission' to export the political, economic, and social systems that have worked so well in the United States to the rest of the world.[6] Consistent with the liberal influence in American policy, global meliorist foreign policy prefers to address the causes of conflict through democracy promotion, defense of human rights, and fostering economic growth, rather than resorting to alleviation of symptomatic discord through belligerent

---

[2] Ashraf Ghani and Clare Lockhart, *Fixing Failed States: A Framework for Rebuilding a Fractured World*, (New York: Oxford University Press, 2009),

[3] Thomas P.M. Barnett, *The Pentagon's New Map: War and Peace in the 21st Century*, (New York: Berkley Books, 2004), 299-301.

[4] Joseph Nye, *Soft Power: The Means to Success in World Politics*, (New York: Public Affairs, 2004), 99 & 105.

[5] Christopher Layne, *The Peace of Illusions*, (Ithaca, NY: Cornell University Press, 2006), 140.

[6] Walter A. McDougall, Promised Land, Crusader State: The American Encounter with the World since 1776, (New York: Houghton Mifflin Company, 1997), 20-21.

application of national power, especially military, as a method of last resort.[7] Global meliorism is based on the conviction that the phenomena that threaten U.S. national interests are the products of oppression and poverty. The latest manifestation of global meliorism is 'smart power', which is the simultaneous use soft and hard power to achieve national objectives, rather than viewing the military as the option of last resort.

The increased focus on non-military elements of national power in American foreign policy has led to a commensurate increase in demand for civil affairs operations in support of country teams and combatant commanders. This monograph reviews existing literature on contemporary civil affairs; highlights the linkage between national strategy, doctrine and force requirements; analyzes demand for reserve and active duty civil affairs forces, proposes a macro-level demand model for determining special operations civil affairs force structure, compares current force structure to the modeled demand, and recommends changes in force structure to meet the demands of persistent conflict for the next two decades. Templated relationship demand is analyzed for reserve component support to conventional forces. The limits of micro-environmental demand in determining special operations force structure are discussed before presenting a macro-level environmental demand model to guide development of active component force structure. The conclusion of this research is that the Department of Defense should increase and realign the force structure of the reserve and active components civil affairs; split the U.S. Army Civil Affairs and Psychological Operations Command into the U.S. Army Civil Affairs Command and the U.S. Army Psychological Operations Command, and move the new two-star headquarters back to the active component under U.S. Army Special Operations Command.

---

[7] Walter A. McDougall, Promised Land, Crusader State: The American Encounter with the World since 1776, (New York: Houghton Mifflin Company, 1997), 208.

Civil Affairs Requirements and Capabilities Literature Review

A review of the existing literature on civil affairs force structure and employment reveals several important points. Prior to 2004, very little was written about civil affairs other than history of Civil Affairs in World War Two, Korea, Vietnam, and Desert Storm. Since 2004, the majority of the literature has been written by current or former civil affairs officers, mostly in the reserve component. While several monographs and articles address the need for a larger civil affairs force structure, none of the authors articulated a methodical way of calculating demand on which to base changes. In 2009, the Center for Strategic & International Studies published a literature review of current civil affairs articles, dating back to 1994, focused on current and future civil affairs requirements and capabilities. The research for this monograph also uncovered several more recent works that are also germane to this analysis.

In early 2004, Lawrence J. Kolb, former Assistant Secretary of Defense for Manpower, Reserve Affairs, Installations, and Logistics from 1981 to 1985, identified that the existing distribution of civil affairs forces between the active and reserve components was inadequate for enduring operations. Korb's opinion piece from the March-April 2004 *Foreign Affairs* is useful to this analysis because it is the first document to present numbers for a proposed shift of civil affairs personnel from the reserve component to the active component. His conclusion is that the underlying assumptions of the All Volunteer Force concept are no longer valid, especially that "essentially civilian functions…would be needed only for postwar stabilization…30 years ago, few imagined that the U.S. military would be used extensively for [peacekeeping] operations." In addition to issues of mobilization procedure, Korb highlights that many of the reservists called up on short notice and extended on their tours are first responders, significantly impacting a homeland security mission also not prevalently envisioned even a decade ago. To sustain the civil affairs requirements in Iraq and Afghanistan alone requires 2000 personnel. Korb advocates for moving 3500 civil affairs positions, approximately two-thirds of the total civil affairs force, to the active component. The implication is that this force level would permit a one-to-one ratio of deployed time to dwell time at home station. [8]

At about the same time, in March 2004, Lieutenant Colonel R.C. Brewer published his U.S. Army War College Strategy Research Project titled, "U.S. Army Civil Affairs and the Fate of Reserve Special Operations Forces in Support of Current and Future Operations." Lieutenant Colonel Brewer's thesis was that reserve component civil affairs forces will be unable to sustain their support for the Global War on Terrorism, plus other demands outside the theaters of war, unless the United States' government implements legal and administrative changes, and restructures civil affairs forces to meet the demands of persistent operations. The primary focus was on the reserve component, but it did also advocate for an increase in active component civil affairs strength. He noted that during major wars, the reserve component will stand and deliver, but that sustaining reserve component support for an extended period of time is problematic because of legal call-up and deployment limitations. He also addressed retention, which is a euphemism for employer and family support. He concluded that the civil affairs community cannot sustain the level of support it had in the previous three years since 2001.

Then Major Darrell W. Martin submitted a thesis to the Command and General Staff College for the Master of Military Arts and Science in early 2004, in which he argued that U.S. Army Civil Affairs forces should be restructured almost exclusively in the active component, including trained civil affairs personnel in maneuver units down to the battalion level.[9] The thesis is included in this literature review only because it accurately assesses the impacts of the high operational tempo of reserve civil affairs forces and it is representative of one line of thinking on how to restructure Civil Affairs. The author noted that at one point in 2004 ninety-one percent of the reserve civil affairs units (brigades and below) were deployed, "there is no hope of a rotation schedule, which allows any sense of normalcy for civilian commercial

---

[8] Lawrence J. Kolb, "Fixing the Mix," *Foreign Affairs* 83, no. 2 (March 2004), 2-7. *Military & Government Collection*, EBSCOhost (accessed January 23, 2010).

[9] Darrell W. Martin, "The Restructuring of the United States Army Civil Affairs," MMAS Thesis, (Fort Leavenworth, KS: Command and General Staff College, 2004), 35.

employers" to rely on reservist employees.[10] Major Martin does advocate bringing civil affairs forces into the active component "and use them like the valuable and limited force multiplier that they are,"[11] although he recommends civil affairs positions be allocated to maneuver units as additional duties for noncommissioned officers. With respect to the only active component civil affairs battalion, he was noncommittal about growth of the unit, but advocated for reducing the unit's mission set.[12] In fairness to the author, there was a dearth of written material from which to conduct an analysis, and the thesis relied heavily on interviews with officers from varied backgrounds, many of whom likely were not familiar with civil affairs or civil military operations doctrine. The work exhibited some lack of understanding, and resultant misrepresentation, of the history of U.S. Army Civil Affairs. The discussion of civil affairs forces structure, manning, training, and equipping is either superficial or displays ignorance with respect to both active component and reserve component units.

Lieutenant Colonel Mark Kimmey's 2005 *Army* magazine article called for radical restructuring of Civil Affairs. Kimmey's thesis was that civil affairs forces must be restructured, retrained, and re-equipped to keep pace with evolving supported forces, and accomplish the emerging mission to build nations in the wake of conflict. The essence of his argument was that reserve civil affairs forces are unable or unwilling to meet long-term commitment, their mandate is too broad, they are poorly equipped to accomplish their missions, and that the U.S. Army Civil Affairs and Psychological Operations Command (USACAPOC), the controlling headquarters for civil affairs forces, is doing a poor job of providing leadership to the Civil Affairs branch. Lieutenant Colonel Kimmey's recommendations included moving "most if not all civil affairs slots from the reserve to the active component…refocus[ing]

---

[10] Ibid., 21.

[11] Ibid., 66.

[12] Ibid., 36-37.

the civil affairs mission away…from Peace Corps-like missions, overhaul the tables of organization and equipping," and changing the civil affairs training and education process.[13]

In 2008, Robert Martinage of the Center for Strategic and Budgetary Assessments (CSBA) research institute published a report titled "Special Operations Forces: Future Challenges and Opportunities" as part of CSBA's Strategy for the Long Haul Series. His thesis was that the Obama Administration should expedite recommended actions of the 2006 Quadrennial Defense Review (QDR) and further expand the structure and capabilities of Special Operations Forces (SOF) to conduct irregular warfare in the emerging global security environment.[14] Martinage concurred with the 2006 Quadrennial Defense Review's (QDR) assessment of the strategic environment and the national interest in failed and failing states. In this environment, "SOF will need to shift from an episodic deployment force to a persistent-presence force – with more forces forward, in more places, for longer periods of time."[15] Martinage noted that the 2006 QDR "launched several important initiatives to better prepare SOF for the future security environment, it fell short in a number of areas…for the U.S. Army Special Operations Command (USASOC), it is imperative to…increase civil affairs and psychological operations force structure."[16] He asserted that the QDR-directed growth is insufficient and recommends that the United States Army expand active component civil affairs forces to four brigades, consisting of sixteen active component battalions.[17] While Martinage has clearly thought at some length about the appropriate civil affairs force structure to meet requirements, he does not lay out his analysis leading to his conclusion.

---

[13] Mark L. Kimmey, "Transforming Civil Affairs," *Army* 55, no. 3 (Mar 2005), http://www3.ausa.org/ webint/DeptArmyMagazine.nsf/byid/KGRG-6CUQGK (accessed Dec 1, 2009).

[14] Robert Martinage, "Special Operations Forces: Future Challenges and Opportunities," (Washington, D.C.: Center for Strategic and Budgetary Assessments, 2008), xiii.

[15] Ibid., 41.

[16] Ibid., 45.

[17] Ibid., 54.

The title of Major Dominic Kusumoto's Air Command and Staff research report, "What should USSOCOM's Active Duty Civil Affairs Force Structure Look Like in the 21st Century?" appears to address the same issue as this monograph. However, that is not the case, as Kusumoto focuses his analysis on the proponent's responsibility for standardizing training across the services' civil affairs forces and placing increased emphasis on skills required for joint and interagency operations. Specifically, he sought to answer the question of "whether or not civil affairs units from different services and training backgrounds can work in a joint interagency environment with a common lexicon of doctrinal terms, baseline training expectations, and skill sets.[18] In his conclusion, Kusumoto supports continuing the status quo, with the U.S. Army John F. Kennedy Special Warfare Center as the proponent for Army Civil Affairs, and the U.S. Army as the DOD executive agent for civil affairs. He also advocates for standardized training across the services and reserves, as well as required experience and Joint training for assignment to general officer commands.[19] While Kusumoto does address organizational culture issues that have resulted from the 2005 DOD-directed move of reserve civil affairs forces to the U.S. Army Reserve Command and differing training, he does not specifically propose a force structure for the 21st Century.

In January 2009, Kathleen Hicks and Christine Wormuth of the Center for Strategic and International Studies published "The Future of U.S. Civil Affairs: A Report of the CSIS International Security Program," for the Office of the Under Secretary of Defense for Policy. DOD commissioned the external comprehensive analysis of civil affairs structure, functions, capabilities, and requirements to prepare a response to the House Armed Services Committee (HASC), addressed in the next paragraph. DOD asked CSIS to examine 10 issue areas, addressing topics such as anticipated civil affairs requirements, suitability of programmed force structure to meet demands, which included an analysis of

---

[18] Dominic Kusumoto, "What should USSOCOM's Active Duty Civil Affairs Force Structure Look Like in the 21st Century?" (Maxwell Air Force Base, AL: Air Command and Staff College, 2008), 1-2.

[19] Ibid., 26-29.

whether or not the active component-reserve component mix is appropriate, whether or not training and competencies are sufficient, and issues pertaining to proponency and personnel management.[20] The authors' thesis was that Civil Affairs should be fully integrated as a branch in the United States Army, with its own proponency and representation at all levels – from tactical to strategic – in Army and Joint headquarters. Specific recommendations relevant to the current analysis were (1) to reintegrate all civil affairs forces as SOF under USASOC under a 1- or 2-star active Civil Affairs general officer, (2) integrate active civil affairs at all levels and incorporate specialization in the active component, (3) create a direct commission authority so DOD can access advanced functional specialists.[21] They conclude that:

> Department of Defense leaders must begin to treat civil affairs forces and civil-military operations as integral to the nation's success across the range of military operations. Civil affairs forces should be in the vanguard of unified civilian and military operations to assist foreign government in preventing security threats from arising and mitigating the effects of state fragility and failure when threats emerge…Today, however, the quality and utility of civil affairs forces are significantly impaired by high operational tempo, insufficient training, poor personnel initiatives, inadequate resourcing and authorities, and lack of advocacy at the Department's highest levels.[22]

While the CSIS report contributes significantly to awareness of issues facing the civil affairs community, the glaring omission is a specific discussion of current and future requirements and the specific structure and capabilities required to meet the demands for civil affairs operations.

The Department of Defense submitted a "Report to Congress on Civil Affairs" in April 2009, responding to the House Armed Services Committee's (HASC) Report 110-652 that accompanied the Fiscal Year 2009 National Defense Authorization Act requesting that the Secretary of Defense analyze and report on civil affairs roles and requirements throughout the spectrum of conflict.[23] The first, second,

---

[20] Kathleen H. Hicks and Christine E. Wormuth, "The Future of U.S. Civil Affairs: A Report of the CSIS International Security Program," (Washington, D.C.: Center for Strategic and International Studies, 2009), viii-ix.

[21] Ibid., vi-vii.

[22] Ibid., 45-46.

[23] Office of the Assistant Secretary of Defense for Special Operations, Low Intensity Conflict & Interdependent Capabilities, "Report to Congress on Civil Affairs," (Washington, D.C: Department of Defense, 2009), 3.

and fifth responses bear directly on the current analysis. The report is remarkable for its lack of data and its failure to directly answer the HASC's questions. In response to the Committee's request for "an analysis of the overall anticipated civil affairs requirement, with a description of how the requirement was determined," the authors' response refers vaguely to the Department's requirement to maintain civil affairs capability, discusses the active component to reserve component ratio, and outlines the Army's expansion of civil affairs force structure through 2013. The response neither provides a basis for determining force structure requirements, nor does it specify what force structure is required to support ongoing Operations Iraqi Freedom and Enduring Freedom, as well as supporting irregular warfare requirements globally. It does not even state that the existing or already approved force structure is adequate.[24] In response to the HASC's second question, "whether the programmed force structure will meet the anticipated requirement," the Department of Defense responded with a partial answer, acknowledging that "projected demand [for civil affairs forces] continues to outpace supply," resulting in the Army's inability to meet prescribed dwell ratios set by the Secretary of Defense for active or reserve civil affairs personnel.[25] The approved Program Change proposal that will add twenty reserve component civil affairs companies and thirty active component companies to the branch end strength, and will allow the Department to meet the Secretary's prescribed dwell ratios by 2013.[26] The response fails to address, at least directly, the persistent global engagement requirements that are the primary missions for the active component. In response to the HASC's fifth question, "whether the current and planned force mix between the active and reserve components is appropriate given the continued demands for civil affairs units," the Department does not directly answer the question, but responds that it "will continually analyze the appropriate active/reserve force mix as the Army implements the force structure changes."[27]

---

[24] Ibid., 6-8.

[25] Ibid., 10.

[26] Ibid., 10.

[27] Ibid., 18.

National Strategies, Quadrennial Reviews, and Doctrine

I believe that American leadership has been wanting, but is still wanted. We must use what has been called "smart power": the full range of tools at our disposal – diplomatic, economic, military, political, legal, and cultural – picking the right tool or combination of tools, for each situation.[28]

Since the United States emerged as a world superpower after World War Two, there are three vital U.S. national interests that have remained unchanged. The first is maintaining the security – the existence – of the United States, as embodied in the Constitution and other public law, against foreign and domestic threats. The second national interest is sustaining the economic prosperity of the state and "facilitating the cooperation of those states that serve this vital interest. Third is…maintaining the stability of the world."[29] Democracy promotion is specifically a means to achieving the United States' third national interest, which has second- and third-order effects on the first two interests. In short, while ways and means have changed over the years as administrations transferred power, the ends have remained the same.

The George H.W. Bush Administration

The 1991 National Security Strategy of the United States addressed the evaporation of the Soviet threat, as well as the associated control of Soviet satellites and allies. The impending collapse of the Soviet Union, based on the successful grand strategy of containment over the previous forty years, dictated the establishment of new policies and a new grand strategy to guide foreign policy in a new era.[30] While the Bush Administration pursued a more liberal agenda in terms of diplomacy and economic interactions, the military's role continued to be primarily coercive, deterring actors that might challenge

---

[28] U.S. Secretary of State, "Statement before the Senate Foreign Relations Committee," Nomination Hearing, January 13, 2009. http://www.state.gov/secretary/rm/2009a/01/115196.htm, (accessed March 22, 2010).

[29] Richard Nere, "Democracy Promotion and the U.S. National Security Strategy: U.S. National Interest, U.S. Primacy, and Coercion," *Strategic Insights* 8, no. 3 (August 2009), http://www.nps.edu/Academics/centers/ccc/publications/OnlineJournal/2009/Aug/nereAug09.pdf (accessed Dec 1, 2009).

[30] U.S. President, *The National Security Strategy of the United States*, (Washington, DC: GPO, 1991), 5.

the new liberal world order and punishing those that failed to play by the new rules of the international relations game.[31] "In the realm of military strategy, we confront[ed] dangers more ambiguous than those we previously faced…to combat not a particular, poised enemy but the nascent threats of power vacuums and regional instabilities."[32] The defense agenda for the 1990s focused on nuclear deterrence, forward presence, and crisis response while simultaneously downsizing and reconstituting U.S. military forces which were still tasked with being capable of defeating the United States' future enemies.

Two specific components – engagement and reserve forces roles and functions – of the defense agenda are significant in our analysis of civil affairs employment. First, engagement, as discussed in the NSS, refers almost exclusively to military-to-military cooperation. In the discussion of "forward presence," the NSS notes that "maintaining a positive influence in distant regions requires that we demonstrate our engagement" with our allies because "our presence can deter aggression, preserve regional balances, deflect arms races and prevent the power vacuums that invite conflict."[33] With respect to "The Rest of the World," the strategy was to create a network of alliances and set conditions for the employment of military force, if required to enforce cooperation with United States' interests.[34] Second, as the United States pared down its forces to the Base Force, there would be an increasing reliance on "reserve support units in any extended confrontation. The primary focus of reserve combat units will be to supplement active units in any especially large or protracted deployment."[35] While liberalism dominated the Bush approach to foreign policy, the military continued to serve primarily as the 'stick' in a 'carrot and stick' approach to foreign relations.

---

[31] Ibid., 3-5.

[32] Ibid., 2.

[33] Ibid., 29.

[34] Ibid., 30.

[35] Ibid., 31 & 34. The Base Force was a minimum active and reserve force that could serve as a basis for rapid mobilization to meet a large scale threat.

The 1992 National Military Strategy (NMS) issued by General Colin Powell did little to further explicate the ways and means to achieving the ends and ways promulgated in the NSS. The Chairman of the Joint Chiefs of Staff regurgitated the ends and means laid out in the NSS before laying out a series of strategic principles and providing guidance for drawing down forces after the Gulf War. In the end, Powell asserts that while the world has changed, the national military strategy remains largely unchanged other than a regional focus, instead of focusing on a global monolith. The military strategy remained to have "forces ready to move either from [the continental United States] or forward deployed locations to the scene of a crisis, have the strategic agility to mass overwhelming force and terminate conflict swiftly and decisively."[36]

The Clinton Administration

The Clinton Administration did not publish its first National Security Strategy until February 1995; however President Clinton directed Les Aspin, after confirmation as the Secretary of Defense, to initiate a comprehensive review of the Department's requirements, strategy, missions, and forces in a Bottom-Up Review that would later become formalized as the Quadrennial Defense Review (QDR). The output of the review was the precursor to the current National Defense Strategy (NDS). The assessment of the strategic environment did not discern any additional threats or opportunities not already identified in the 1992 NSS.[37] However, the Bottom-Up Review did outline Global Cooperative Initiatives, which sought to expand the Defense Department's planning and capabilities for peacekeeping and peace enforcement, humanitarian assistance and disaster/famine relief, and democracy promotion as part of an interagency effort.[38] The Global Cooperation Initiatives set the foundation for a military strategy of

---

[36] Joint Chiefs of Staff, *National Military Strategy of the United States*, (Washington, DC: Joint Chiefs of Staff, 1992), 26.

[37] Department of Defense, *Report on the Bottom-Up Review*, (Washington, D.C.: Department of Defense, 1993), 1-2.

[38] Ibid., 75.

multilateralism. Addressing reserve component forces, the review envisioned "reserve forces [helping] promote international stability and security during peacekeeping, peace enforcement, and humanitarian operations...During prolonged operations...reserve forces are available to provide a rotational or replacement base."[39] The review did not envision routine extended deployment of reserve forces, such as civil affairs, outside of war or contingency operations. In many ways, the Bottom-Up Review fed the Administrations first national security strategy.

In 1995, the Clinton Administration published *A National Security Strategy of Engagement and Enlargement.* The security strategy was reflective of a new grand strategy, that of global hegemony. While many refuted, and continue to do so, the hegemonic aspirations of the United States out of political correctness, President Clinton's preface to the NSS noted "our extraordinary diplomatic leverage to reshape existing security and economic structures...our economic strength gives us a position of advantage on almost every global issue...[and] military force remains an indispensible element of our national power."[40] Invoking the devastating results of American isolationism in the interwar period between the World Wars, Clinton announced a strategy that called for U.S. leadership primarily through diplomatic and economic engagement to enlarge the community of democratic states. The strategy emphasized multilateral military enforcement of political resolutions, but left open the option of unilateral action.

Whether conducted to achieve national security interests as asserted by the Clinton White House or global meliorism as charged by critics, there is no disputing that the Administration expanded both unilateral and multilateral engagement.[41] "At any given time, [the DOD had] small teams of military experts deployed in roughly 25 countries helping host governments" counter subversion, lawlessness, or

---

[39] Ibid., 90.

[40] U.S. President, A *National Security Strategy* of Engagement and Enlargement, (Washington, DC: GPO, 1995), ii.

[41] Ibid., 17.

insurgency.[42] "Engagement and humanitarian assistance were designed to promote human rights, alleviate suffering, and establish democratic regimes with stable economies in order to stem the flow of migration and reduce refugee crises.[43] The employment of special operations forces to conduct these missions was dictated by three basic categories of national interests: vital national interests, important national interests, and humanitarian interests. The implication was that these scarce resources must be focused where the United States has the greatest stake.[44] "Multilateral peace operations were an important component of our strategy. From traditional peacekeeping to peace enforcement, multilateral peace operations [were] viewed] sometimes the best way to prevent, constrain, or resolve conflicts..."[45] The radical changes in ways and means laid out in the NSS caused a radical rewriting of the 1995 National Military Strategy.

The 1995 National Military Strategy represented a significant shift in the ways the military accomplished the strategic ends outlined in the NSS and the NMS. Most notably, "promote stability" was established as a national military objective alongside "thwart aggression" and "peacetime engagement" was added as a co-equal component, or way, of achieving strategic ends alongside "deterrence and conflict prevention, and fighting and winning our nation's wars."[46] The NMS noted that in the years since the Berlin Wall came down, the U.S. military [had] "deployed...to assist in security or humanitarian crises about forty times – a far greater pace than in the preceding 20 years."[47] The strategy specifically stated that the Department of Defense intended to use the Armed Forces to conduct daily, peacetime activities to promote stability and foster democracy. The Department of Defense would leverage assets,

---

[42] Ibid., 11.

[43] Ibid., 24.

[44] Ibid., 12-13.

[45] Ibid., 16.

[46] Joint Chiefs of Staff, *National Military Strategy* of the United States of America 1995: A *Strategy* of Flexible and Selective Engagement, (Washington, DC: Joint Chiefs of Staff, 1995), i.

[47] Ibid., 2.

capabilities, and skills to respond to emerging regional instabilities.[48] In outlining peacetime engagement, the NMS specifically addresses civil-military operations under nation assistance, and addresses capabilities that Civil Affairs provide in other operations.[49] The NMS, for the first time, also addresses post conflict, civil military operations to re-establish stability and "win the peace."[50] A significant outcome of the 1995 NMS was the creation of the DOD's theater engagement planning process, first approved by the President in 1997.[51]

The next strategy document to influence Civil Affairs' roles and missions was the National Security Strategy published in December 1999.[52] The *National Security Strategy for a New Century* placed greater emphasis on transnational threats and failed states, asserting that "our citizens have a direct and increasing stake in the prosperity and stability of other nations, in their support for international norms and human rights, in their ability to combat international crime."[53] The Strategy called for preventative approaches to maintaining stability because they are more cost effective economically, politically and socially than crisis response.[54] Two areas of increased emphasis in the NSS were terrorist sanctuaries overseas and sustainable development to reduce the attraction of terrorist organizations and international organized crime, including the illegal drug trade.[55]

---

[48] Ibid., 4-5.

[49] Ibid., 8-9.

[50] Ibid., 16.

[51] U.S. President, *A National Security Strategy for a New Century*, (Washington, DC: GPO, 1999), 11.

[52] The 1997 QDR and the 1997 National Military Strategy focused on emerging kinetic threats, conventional force structure for 2010, and continued reduction and realignment of the Armed Forces. The documents did not present any changes that significantly impact this analysis.

[53] *A National Security Strategy for a New Century*, 1-2.

[54] Ibid., 6.

[55] Ibid., 14 & 25 .

The George H. Bush Administration

> The Bush Doctrine was indeed the United States' national security strategy, under which, to achieve security in an insecure world, the United States relied on three fundamental pillars: preventative war, unilateralism, and regime change. It was, in fact, a more aggressive and proactive foreign policy strategy relative to the national security strategies of previous Administrations.[56]

Although the 2001 Quadrennial Defense Review came on the heal of the September 11, 2001 attacks in New York and Washington, D.C., the report was already complete at the time of the attacks, and does not represent a specific response to them.[57] The 2001 QDR marked a Department of Defense paradigm shift away from engagement outside traditional military-to-military contacts, to refocus the DOD primarily on military power. The Review notes that diplomatic and economic efforts seek to promote [peace, freedom, and prosperity] globally by encouraging democracy and free markets. U.S. defense strategy seeks to defend freedom for the United States and its allies and friends, and it helps to secure an international environment of peace that makes other goals possible.[58]

Two findings of the QDR are of interest for this analysis. First, in assessing the strategic environment, the Review noted *"increasing challenges and threats emanating from the territories of weak and failing states.* The absence of capable or responsible governments in many countries…creates a fertile ground for non-state actors engaging" in both domestic and transnational drug trafficking, terrorism, and other illegal activities that threaten security and stability.[59] The QDR also found that the "readiness of the Army's highest priority units [had] been sustained at the expense of non-divisional and Reserve Component units and the institutional Army."[60]

---

[56] Nere, "Democracy Promotion and the U.S. National Security Strategy: U.S. National Interest, U.S. Primacy, and Coercion."

[57] Department of Defense, *Quadrennial Defense Review Report*, (Washington, D.C.: Department of Defense, 2001), iii.

[58] Ibid., 11.

[59] Ibid., 5.

[60] Ibid., 8.

The 2002 National Security Strategy focuses almost exclusively on the foreign policy ends and ways, often defaulting to a whole of government approach to achieving security – especially defeating terrorism – regaining economic prosperity, and promoting democracy. The 2004 National Military Strategy allocates means to accomplish the objectives of the NSS. The 2004 NMS establishes stability operations as a critical component of achieving national military objectives and setting conditions for success by the other elements of national power. Joint operating concepts (JOCs), under development when the NMS was published included stability operations.[61] Under the national military objective of protecting the United States, the Armed Forces will:

> Create a global anti-terrorism environment…our strategy will diminish the conditions that permit terrorism to flourish. To defeat terrorists we will support national and partner nation efforts to deny state sponsorship, support, and sanctuary to terrorist organizations. We will work to deny terrorists safe haven in failed states and ungoverned regions.[62]

The NMS objective of preventing conflict and surprise attacks noted that:

> Preventing conflict requires the capability to perform stability operations to maintain or re-establish order, promote peace and security or improve existing conditions…Such actions reduce the underlying conditions that foster terrorism and the extremist ideologies that support terrorism. Stability operations create favorable security conditions that allow other instruments of national and international power to succeed.[63]

The military objective of prevailing against adversaries emphasized:

> Winning decisively will require synchronizing and integrating major combat operations, stability operations and significant post-conflict interagency operations to establish conditions of stability and security favorable to the United States…The JOCs for major combat operations and stability operations are complementary and must be fully integrated and synchronized in campaign planning.[64]

The 2005 National Defense Strategy is reflective of Administration efforts, especially by Secretary of Defense Rumsfeld, to transfer diplomatic and economic tasks to the Department of State in

---

[61] Joint Chiefs of Staff, The *National Military Strategy* of the United States of America: A *Strategy* for Today, a Vision for Tomorrow, (Washington, DC: Joint Chiefs of Staff, 2004), 9.

[62] Ibid., 10-11.

[63] Ibid., 13.

[64] Ibid., 14.

order to focus on the development and employment of military combat power to achieve national objectives. The relevant developments in this NDS are the acknowledgement of the need to train for sustained stability operations – including language capabilities and Civil-military Affairs capabilities – and cooperation with the Department of State Office of the Coordinator for Reconstruction and Stabilization (S/CRS). The latter initiative was supported by DOD because "[its] intent [was] to focus our efforts on those tasks most directly associated with establishing favorable long-term security conditions."[65]

Between 2005 and 2008, changes in national strategy focused on areas with minimal impact on civil affairs forces. The one significant outcome of the 2006 QDR was the creation of the 95th Civil Affairs Brigade and authorization for the first four expansion battalions.[66] However, in 2008 the pendulum swung back to DOD performance of military engagement with publication of the 2008 National Defense Strategy.

The 2008 National Defense Strategy published by Robert Gates emphasized the need to develop a broad mastery of irregular warfare comparable to our traditional dominance in conventional combat. A new emphasis is placed on non-lethal components of irregular warfare that "promote local participation in government and economic programs to spur development, as well as efforts to understand and address grievances that often lie at the heart of insurgencies."[67] The Department of Defense, in partnership with other government agencies and international actors will work to improve conditions and address root causes of turmoil to undermine support for insurgencies and terrorism, and stabilize threatened areas.

---

[65] Ibid., 15-16.

[66] Department of Defense, *Quadrennial Defense Review Report*, (Washington, D.C.: Department of Defense, 2006), 5.

[67] Department of Defense, *National Defense Strategy*, (Washington, DC: Department of Defense, 2008), 8.

The Obama Administration

As of March 2010, the Obama administration has yet to publish a National Security Strategy, matching the longest period without a change of NSS since 1991, shortly after the end of the Cold War. The Department of Defense has yet to publish updated National Military Strategy or a National Defense Strategy since President Obama was inaugurated. Strategy and policy in the absence of published guidance is discerned from public speeches and writings. Washington Post journalist E.J. Dionne, Jr. has described the 'Obama Doctrine' as "a form of realism unafraid to deploy power but mindful that its use must be tempered by practical limits and a dose of self-awareness."[68] Some critics characterized candidate Obama's foreign policy approach as pacifist based on his comment during an Associated Press interview on July 21, 2007, in which he stated "the United States cannot use its military to solve humanitarian problems and that preventing a potential genocide in Iraq isn't a good enough reason to keep U.S. forces there." The comment is indicative of a president that is not a global meliorist. Neither does the President appear to be an exceptionalist based on his comment to a reporter in France that equated American exceptionalism with every other nation's and his apologetic interview on Arab Al Arabiya network.[69] In his address at West Point, President Obama reaffirmed the United States' commitment to Afghanistan and Pakistan because "our security is at stake" in the region.[70] The President outlined using all elements of national power to achieve American strategic goals. These principles have been echoed and reinforced by the Secretaries of State and Defense, as well as senior leaders in the Department of Defense.

President Obama advocates the balanced application of soft and hard power to achieve U.S. strategic objectives. Secretary Clinton, in her confirmation for Secretary of State used the term 'smart

---

[68] E.J. Dionne, Jr., "The Obama Doctrine in Action," *Washington Post*, April 16, 2009. http://www.washington post.com/wp-dyn/content/article/2009/04/5/AR2009041502902.html, (accessed Mar 22, 2010).

[69] James Kirchick, "Squanderer in chief," *Los Angeles Times,* April 28, 2009. http://articles.latimes.com/ 2009/apr/28/opinion/oe-kirchick28, (accessed March 25, 2010).

[70] U.S. President, "Remarks by the President in Address to the Nation on the Way Forward in Afghanistan and Pakistan," (Address, West Point, NY, December 1, 2009)

power.'[71] Smart power is the judicious application of soft power and hard power, simultaneously if needed, both directly and indirectly. Unlike soft power, military force is not viewed as the option of last resort, and unlike purer realism, neither is it the first option. Most importantly, it is not an 'either...or', but a 'what is most appropriate whole of government approach'? Secretary of Defense Robert Gates has emphasized the importance of non-military elements of national power in his speeches and budgeting. An advocate of preparing for hybrid warfare – a blend of conventional and unconventional warfare – Gates believes that simultaneous application of all elements of national power in some manner is the appropriate way to resolve conflict.[72] Addressing the International Institute for Strategic Studies, Gates noted that the United States will be "more collaborative and consultative [in] foreign policy...will continue to be assertive on the international stage...[and] will protect our allies and our interests."[73]

On February 1, 2010, the Department of Defense released the Quadrennial Defense Review. One of the significant changes is the elimination of the requirement for the United States' Armed Forces to be prepared to fight two major wars simultaneously.[74] The Armed Forces will be sized to prevail in Afghanistan, Iraq, and against Al Qaeda in the near term, as well as defeat another regional aggressor and support civil authorities to defend the homeland. In the medium- to long-term, the military must be able to 1) conduct a stabilization operation, defeat a highly capable regional aggressor, and provide support to civil authorities; or 2) defeat two regional aggressors and maintain a heightened state of readiness in defense of the homeland; or 3) conduct a stabilization operation, a long-term regional deterrence,

---

[71] U.S. Secretary of State, "Statement before the Senate Foreign Relations Committee," Nomination Hearing, January 13, 2009. http://www.state.gov/secretary/rm/2009a/01/115196.htm, (accessed March 22, 2010).

[72] U.S. Secretary of Defense, Speech to the Association of the United States Army, Washington, D.C., October 5, 2009. http://www.defense.gov/speeches/speech.aspx?speechid=1357, (accessed March 23, 2010).

[73] U.S. Secretary of Defense, Speech to the International Institute for Strategic Studies, Singapore, Indonesia, May 30, 2009. http://www.defense.gov/speeches/speech.aspx?speechid=1383, (accessed March 23, 2010).

[74] Jordan Reimer, "Review Drops Two-War Force Size Paradigm," *American Forces Press Service*, (March 10, 2010). http://www.defense.gov/news/newsarticle.aspx?id=58273, (accessed March 27, 2010).

counterinsurgency in a nation, and provide support to civil authorities.[75] The emphasis on stability

operations and support to civil authorities is a significant expansion of engagement initiated in previous

QDRs. The QDR report notes that civil affairs forces are one of the many critical enablers that have been

persistently short.[76] In addition to their traditional missions, the report emphasizes civil affairs support of

whole-of-government stability, support, transition and reconstruction operations, especially provincial

reconstruction teams and human terrain teams. The report highlights the previously approved and ongoing

expansion, but does not imply any additional civil affairs growth.[77]

Civil Affairs Doctrine since the Cold War

Military doctrine is a commonly understood body of principles for the employment of armed

forces. Doctrine is not strategy, but the result of strategy, which bridges policy and doctrine.[78] The

American strategy of promoting democracy, advancing free markets, and maximizing global stability

through hard and soft power, seeks to achieve the policy objectives of national security, economic

prosperity, and respect for basic human rights. Whereas strategy represents decisions on how best to

achieve objectives, doctrine is a baseline template that addresses the force structure required to conduct

what types of missions, in what environment and when, to achieve specific effects. Joint civil affairs

doctrine is primarily laid out in Joint Publication (JP) 3-57, *Civil Military Operations* published in 1995,

2001, and 2008; previously a separate Joint Publication 3-57.1, *Civil Affairs* was also published in 2003.

Army civil affairs doctrine is embodied in Field Manual 3-05.40 (formerly Field Manual 41-10), *Civil*

Affairs Operations – published since the Cold War in 1993, 2000, and 2006 – and Field Manual 3-05.401,

---

[75] Department of Defense, "Quadrennial Defense Review and Ballistic Missile Defense Review," (briefing, February 1, 2010), Slide 6. http://www.defense.gov/news/d2010usdprolloutbrief.pdf, (Accessed March 27, 2010).

[76] Department of Defense, *Quadrennial Defense Review Report*, (Washington, D.C.: Department of Defense, 2010), 101.

[77] Ibid., 24-25.

[78] Colin S. Gray, War, Peace and International Relations: An Introduction to Strategic History, (New York: Routledge, 2007), 284.

Civil Affairs Tactics, Techniques and Procedures. This monograph focuses on the Army 'operations'

publications because they address who, what, when, where, why, and how of civil affairs at the

operational and strategic levels and are reflective of the Joint publications.

Army civil affairs doctrine remained largely unchanged from Cold War doctrine during the

George H.W. Bush Administration, and serves as a base for analysis. In the early 1990s, no specific Joint

doctrine existed for the employment of civil affairs forces or the conduct of civil-military operations.[79]

Test Joint Publication 3-07, *Doctrine for Joint Operations in Low Intensity Conflict*, published in 1990

only noted that a number of military activities, including civic actions, humanitarian assistance, and civil

military operations support other government agencies in assisting the stability of friendly governments.[80]

The doctrine emphasizes that the Department of State is responsible for operations other than war,

supported by the Department of Defense. It further asserts that "successful employment of CMO may

reduce or eliminate the need for subsequent combat operations."[81] The existing Army civil affairs

doctrine at the end of the Cold War was published in 1985. Field Manual (FM) 41-10, *Civil Affairs*

Operations, addressed civil affairs support to general purpose forces only in terms of combat support,

including supplementing other intelligence gathering efforts.[82] The third and fourth chapters discuss civil

affairs forces support to Special Forces in the conduct of foreign internal defense and unconventional

warfare operations throughout the spectrum of conflict. The fifth chapter addresses the role of civil affairs

forces in civil administration, from advising existing governments to establishing military government in

---

[79] The development of a Joint Staff and joint doctrine proceeded from the requirements established in the Goldwater-Nichols Act of 1987.

[80] Joint Staff. *Joint Pub 3-07: Doctrine for Joint Operations in Low Intensity Conflict*, (Washington, DC: Joint Staff, 1990), I-6 to I-9. The term low intensity conflict was a new term introduced in Joint Test Pub 3-0 in 1989 as part of the concept of a spectrum of conflict.

[81] Ibid., II-12.

[82] Department of the Army, Field Manual 41-10: *Civil Affairs Operations*, (Washington, DC: GPO, 1985), 2-1 & 1-4.

friendly or occupied territories.[83] The specific mission activities of civil affairs were populace and

resources control (PRC), foreign nation support (FNS), humanitarian assistance (HA), military civic

action (MCA), and civil defense (CD).[84] President Bush significantly altered American strategy in 1992

during an address in Aspen Colorado in which he:

> formally outlined an evolving policy he called 'peacetime engagement.' With the demise
> of the Soviet Union, U.S. strategic focus has changed from bipolar confrontation and the
> possibility of global war to a multipolar world or regional and transregional threats…The
> Secretary of Defense built upon the President's statement, saying that--'To help deter low-
> intensity conflicts and promote stability in the Third World, we must have innovative
> strategies that support representative government, integrate security assistance, and
> promote economic development. Our approach for doing this is peacetime engagement--a
> coordinated combination of political, economic, and military actions, aimed primarily at
> counteracting local violence and promoting nation-building.' Peacetime engagement
> reflects a shift from global to regional crisis management.[85]

The more comprehensive 1993 edition of FM 41-10 was a significant improvement over the 1985

edition, adding chapters on 'civil affairs organization and functions,', and 'command and control', among

many others. Although special operations commands increased deployments in the 1990s, the

conventional force was resistant to engagement outside traditional military-to-military training exchanges,

resulting in the Chairman Joint Chiefs of Staff issuing Memorandum 3113.01: Theater Engagement

Planning, in 1998 to direct combatant command to develop theater engagement plans and brief the DOD

for approval.[86] Additionally, the change in strategy required modification of how reserve component

forces were integrated into engagement plans. The field manual noted challenges to mobilizing reserve

units outside of war were problematic, requiring rotation of many units during annual training for a single

---

[83] Ibid., 1-5.

[84] Definitions and explication of missions is located in the glossary at Appendix A.

[85] Department of the Army, Field Manual 41-10: *Civil Affairs Operations*, (Washington, DC: GPO, 1993), 8-1.

[86] Ralph R. Steinke and Brian L Tarbet, "Theater Engagement Plans: A Strategic Tool or a Waste of Time," *Paramters* 30, no. 1 (Spring 2000), http://www.carlisle.army.mil/usawc/parameters/00spring/steinke.htm, (accessed March 28, 2010)

mission, or filling requirements on a volunteer basis.[87] During the 1990s most civil affairs missions were conducted by active duty forces, with the reserve component filling shortfalls in active capacity and providing functional specialty support.[88] The 2000 edition of FM 41-10 changed very little of the doctrine, being more of a refinement of the text. The next impetus for doctrinal change would be the Global War on Terror.

The 2006 edition of *Civil Affairs Operations* reflects three major changes that stemmed from Army experiences with insurgency after the invasions of Afghanistan and Iraq. First, it adjusted the civil affairs core tasks in support of maneuver commanders. The 2006 doctrine eliminated foreign nation support, military civic action, and civil defense. It added nation assistance, and civil information management. The core task of civil information management (CIM) is the U.S. Army effort to integrate its civil military operations processes with whole-of-government stability operations. While civil affairs forces have always stressed unity of effort with other agencies, CIM represents the integration of emerging technologies to improve information sharing. Support to civil administration became a core task. Second, it reflected the realignment of reserve component forces to USARC. Reserve component civil affairs were redesignated general purpose forces in support of maneuver commanders. Army leaders eliminated specialization of Army Reserve CA battalions – designation as general purpose, direct support or special operations – reflecting not only global changes since the Cold War but also non-SOF status. Third, the active component civil affairs brigade would support SOF. At the same time, the manual noted that "the active Army CA brigade does not have a functional specialty cell like the USAR CA brigade and, therefore, requires augmentation from the USAR CA brigade or CACOM when it requires these skill sets."[89]

---

[87] FM 41-10, 1993, 9-5.

[88] Lecture, Civil Affairs Qualification Course, Fort Bragg, North Carolina, 2005.

[89] Department of the Army, Field Manual 3-05.40: *Civil Affairs Operations*, (Washington, DC: GPO, 2006), 2-18.

The major changes in civil affairs doctrine in the past two decades have been when and where civil affairs forces are employed, and the command and control structure. This monograph asserts that employment has been insufficient and under-resourced. The change in Army Civil Affairs structure has complicated, rather than simplified, support to both conventional and special operations forces.[90] However, civil affairs soldiers perform essentially the same tactical tasks on the ground. Civil affairs units still work to minimize civilian interference with military operations, minimize the impact of military operations on the population, legitimate governments, reduce factors of instability, and isolate insurgents. The civil affairs community is working to advance management of civil information and sharing to improve interagency unity of effort. Demand for civil affairs operations has increased over the past two decades as soft power, and then smart power have increasingly dominated strategy. Unfortunately, Army leaders have been using the wrong type of demand signals to structure the force. Additionally, the shift of RC CA out of special operations eliminated unity of command and confounds unity of effort.

---

[90] Thomas Hartzel, "CA Force Structure Analysis," (briefing, Fort Bragg, NC, 2008), Slide 5.

Demand for Civil Affairs Forces

The most likely situation where U.S. national interests are at stake will occur in situations short of war. Operations short of war, which include peacetime engagement, demand a new proactive planning focus to promote regional stability as a means to deter conflict. By helping [host nations] provide for their own defense needs and develop sustainable responsive institutions, the Army may reduce the likelihood that it will have to deploy to protect threatened U.S. interests. These operations will emphasize the indirect use of forces in roles that support other nations in their efforts to maintain stability, law, and order.[91]

Demand for civil affairs forces can be determined in three ways. The first type, hereafter referred to as templated relationship demand, is based on support relationships in which support units of a particular size support specified echelon maneuver units. A second type of demand, referred to as micro-level environmental demand, is based on specific needs in particular areas and is most useful for developing detailed response packages. A third type of demand, macro level environmental demand, offers to provide a logical basis for developing active component special operations civil affairs units based on observed holistic conditions of states' domestic environment.

Templated relationship demand is useful for building force structure, particularly for maneuver support elements such as reserve component civil affairs, as well as for general force apportionment and allocation, especially for major combat operations. However, its weakness is that it does not account for environmental conditions such as population density, geography, social systems, and threat in the operational environment. Habitual relationship demand as a method is proactive, predictive, and appropriate for determining support structure for conventional forces because it follows a logical pattern.[92] This form of demand will be used in the following sections to analyze reserve component civil affairs ability to support conventional maneuver forces using current habitual relationships. This type of

---

[91] *Field Manual 41-10: Civil Affairs Operations*, (Washington, D.C.: GPO, 1993), 8-1.

[92] The author only asserts that the methodology and logic are appropriate for building conventional force structure. The author does not assert that the current habitual support relationships are adequate to support maneuver units in the contemporary environment.

demand appears to have been the basis for maintaining a civil affairs battalion, with a company aligned with each combatant command and special forces group, in the active component after Vietnam.[93]

In the middle of the past decade, the U.S. Army recognized that the existing active component civil affairs force structure was inadequate for the contemporary environment. The Army compared missions requested to missions it was able to resource with the lone civil affairs battalion, determining that a brigade, with a battalion aligned to each combatant command, would be adequate to fill the majority of mission requests. This is a form of micro-environmental analysis applied to habitual relationships. It appears in the literature that it is precisely this methodology that the United States Army is using to determine active component civil affairs structure for the next decade. Micro-level environmental demand is useful for determining specific mission requirements, but it is reactive and of limited use in building force structure. Furthermore, the calculations needed to determine an appropriate force structure are both cumbersome and highly susceptible to multiple small changes. The Army should be building special operations civil affairs capabilities to meet global threats to stability in the same manner that it builds maneuver forces and special forces structure to counter lethal threats. What is needed is a macro level model that incorporates the proactive and predictive characteristics of the templated relationship model with the situational understanding of the micro-level environmental demand.

Macro-level environmental demand, based on holistic evaluation of states' domestic political, economic, social and infrastructure conditions, offers to provide a logical basis for developing active component special operations civil affairs units. The proposed macro-level analysis eliminates several independent variables from the demand equation, including the personal political views of actors, screening by various organizations, and the limiting effect of a known scarce resource. After considering several existing analyses of fragile states, this paper proposes adopting the most comprehensive. Using

---

[93] Lecture, Civil Affairs Qualification Course, Fort Bragg, North Carolina, 2005.

the list of fragile states as a basis, the author will present an analysis of active component civil affairs forces required to meet demand. An assumption of this macro-level analysis, and an admitted weakness, is that all fragile states require a single civil affairs team to address factors of instability in partnership with the country team. However, a second, mitigating assumption is that not all countries will allow employment of civil affairs inside their borders, freeing up some assets for concentration in priority countries. The reader should keep in mind that the intent of macro-level analysis is to determine the baseline force structure needed to address global instability. Army leadership can apply weighting to specific countries to refine demand. This monograph, after developing a baseline, applies a weight factor of two to the Central Command operating environment. After determining the maximum demand, the Army can apply screening criteria and determine the level of risk leaders are willing to assume.

Civil Affairs Support to Conventional Forces

Civil Affairs support to conventional forces is based on a template as outlined in *Civil Affairs Operations*, the field manual guiding the employment of civil affairs forces. The basic concept for support is that a civil affairs team-alpha (CAT-A) supports a maneuver battalion, a civil affairs company supports a maneuver brigade, a civil affairs battalion supports a division, a civil affairs brigade supports a corps, and a civil affairs command (CACOM) supports a field army or theater command. The more current versions of the field manual allow for variation from the template based on conditions on the ground in the theater of operations.[94] However, in practice, there is very little variation from the doctrinal support template.

---

[94] Field Manual 3-05.40: Civil Affairs Operations, (2006), 2-2.

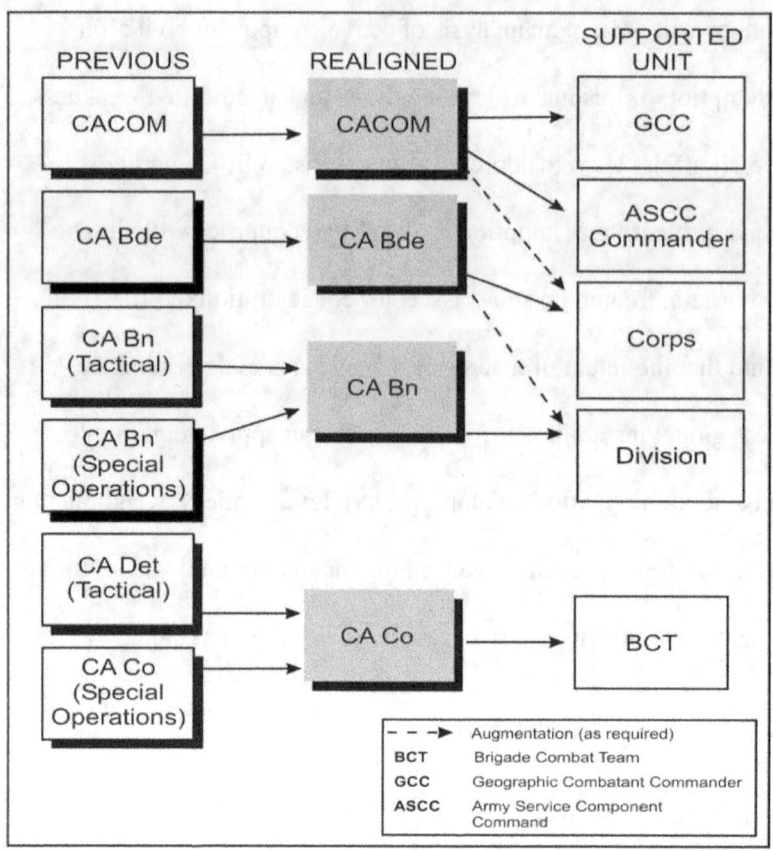

Figure 1: Conventional CA USAR support model (FM 3-05.40, 2006)

Prior to the 2003 invasion of Iraq, real demand for civil affairs support to conventional forces was largely limited to support to the combatant commanders' theater security cooperation plans during peacetime. Peacetime support to bilateral and multilateral exercises was provided primarily through Reserve annual training. Bosnia-Herzegovina and Kosovo, as well as humanitarian assistance missions, generated the majority of operational demand. The demand was well within the capabilities of the force structure resourced to support wartime needs. The basis for civil affairs force structure was its ability to support major combat operations in two major regional conflicts while sustaining theater security cooperation elsewhere.

The doctrinal concept for employment of Civil Affairs in support of conventional land forces was to provide active component civil affairs elements for contingency operations and immediate support for war operations until reserve forces could mobilize and deploy to one or two regional conflicts. The worst case scenario for multiple regional conflicts was a conflict on the Korean Peninsula simultaneous with a conflict in the Middle East, requiring the deployment of all five active duty corps.[95] The first major assumption, based on the collapse of the Soviet Union, was that American and allied air, land, and sea power would rapidly defeat enemy forces. The second assumption was that military operations would quickly transition back to theater security cooperation activities, albeit at a higher level of engagement; the Department of State and the United States Agency for International Development (USAID) would lead stability or reconstruction efforts.[96] Given the preceding assumptions, civil affairs combat support requirements would be approximately five civil affairs brigades with a total of sixty companies, or a total of 300 Civil Affairs teams for a period not to exceed one year. The Korean peninsula would also likely require a civil affairs command. A civil affairs command would be required in another theater only if the land component force exceeded corps size. These planning assumptions remained valid until 2004.

In the aftermath of successful military operations to remove the existing regimes from power in Afghanistan and Iraq, assumptions in both theaters of operation pertaining to conflict termination were largely inaccurate and resulted in extended counterinsurgency operations. Coalition political and military leaders expected that upon removal of the oppressive regimes in both countries, the citizens would coalesce around the diasporas that had lobbied the United States for military action to free their peoples. Many leaders further assumed that the people would naturally form democracies. However, the incumbent regimes dissolved without surrendering and formed insurgencies, intending to wear down the coalitions and regain power. Political and military leaders came to the realization that the United States needed to fill the power vacuum to prevent re-emergence of the regimes and to mitigate instability in the regions. In both cases, Removal of the Ba'ath and Taliban regimes necessitated counterinsurgency

---

[95] Joint Chiefs of Staff, *National Military Strategy of the United States*, (Washington, D.C., 1992), 17-18.

[96] U.S. President, *A National Security Strategy of Engagement and Enlargement*, (Washington, DC: GPO, 1995), ii-iii.

operations and nation-building in order to sustain the nascent governments, an activity the United States had not undertaken successfully since the rebuilding of Europe and Japan after World War Two.[97]

In 2004, a year after U.S. forces ousted the Hussein regime, with forces still in Afghanistan and Iraq, Army leaders, particularly in the special operations community, facing an era of persistent conflict, recognized the need to reassess assumptions and demand for civil affairs forces. From 2004 to 2010, the United States Army has maintained approximately twenty brigade combat teams and maneuver enhancement brigades deployed in the two theaters of operation. The Department of Defense and the U.S. Army has more recently placed greater emphasis on refining the civil affairs force structure to meet support requirements for an era of persistent conflict in which active duty and reserve component forces are envisioned to conduct more expeditionary missions around the globe in support of stability, security, transition and reconstruction (SSTR) operations.[98]

In 2008 the U.S. Army Special Operation Command (USASOC) conducted an analysis of reserve component civil affairs demand and force structure based on the Force Design Update (FDU) 05-01 vision for U.S. Army Reserve concept of support. The guidance was to build sufficient capability to support one civil affairs company for each of 20 deployed brigade combat teams (BCTs) using the doctrinal support template. Operational tempo for the companies is to be one year deployed and five years (1:5) of dwell time at home. The guidance assumed twelve months "boots on the ground" in the theater of operations. The FDU 05-01 total requirement was for 120 companies for a six-year cycle. Between the time FDU 05-01 was issued and USASOC conducted its analysis in 2008, the Department of Defense issued requirements for another ten company equivalents annually to support provincial reconstruction teams, human terrain teams, two companies in the Horn of Africa, and one elsewhere, increasing the total

---

[97] Miguel A. Castellanos, "Civil Affairs – Building the Force to Meet Its Future Challenges," (Carlisle Barracks, PA: U.S. Army War College, 2009) 1. Military governance units were the predecessors of modern day CA units, composed of specially trained governance experts that facilitated European occupation and implementation of the Marshall Plan.

[98] Department of Defense, "Department of Defense Directive 3000.05: Military Support for Stability, Security, transition, and Reconstruction Operations," (Washington, D.C: Department of Defense, 2005), 2.

baseline requirement to 30 companies yearly, or 180 companies for the six-year cycle. However, Congress has limited total mobilization time to twelve months for reservists; subtracting time for mobilization and demobilization means reservists only serve nine months "boots on the ground." Adjusting for only 75% utilization, the six-year requirement for reserve civil affairs totals 240 full strength companies. The preceding calculation represents the ideal based on the FDU 05-01 guidance. USASOC's calculations acknowledged that 1:5 dwell time was not achievable in the near term; utilizing 1:4 dwell time, they obtained a six-year requirement for 200 company equivalents.[99]

Civil Affairs Special Operations

Micro-level environmental demand currently determines requirements for special operations by active component civil affairs teams and the corresponding necessary force structure. In other words, country teams and combatant commands request civil affairs support to meet specific objectives, rather than providing support to maneuver units. Active component elements normally deploy around the globe, conducting operations in support of country teams and combatant commands, as opposed to supporting maneuver units. When civil affairs teams provide support to special forces units, it is normally to the operational or theater strategic command, not the tactical detachments. When civil affairs units provide support to conventional maneuver units, it is normally on a short-term basis until reserve forces can be mobilized and deployed. Active component civil affairs teams provide immediate, short-term generalist civil affairs support to special operation forces and contingency operations forces until replaced by reserve component civil affairs units with functional expertise. Active duty civil affairs soldiers are linguists and culturally attuned to their area of operations, "generalists trained 'to map the civil human

---

[99] Hartzel, "CA Force Structure Analysis," Slide 6.

terrain and then identify the civil vulnerabilities that can be exploited' by terrorists and insurgents in developing nations."[100]

For at least the past decade, demand has exceeded the supply of civil affairs teams. Specific data is limited on the demand for active component civil affairs because of the classified nature of special operations. However, in November 2008, the USASOC staff presented an unclassified brief to the Commander on the Total Army Analysis (TAA) 2010-2015 Civil Affairs and Psychological Operations Approved Growth. The document noted that that for fiscal year 2010 there were 69 mission requests for active component civil affairs ranging in size from two-man civil-military support elements (CMSE) to civil affairs companies, but that the 95th Civil Affairs Brigade could only fill 28 requests. The slide presentation notes that "inventory is inadequate to support current SOF requirements. Contingency support to [general purpose forces] further degrades the ability to resource SOF requirements."[101] One needs to understand that 69 mission requests represents the final demand after filtering through country team processes, theater special operations commands prioritizations, and the U.S. Army Special Operations Command's evaluation of which missions are appropriate SOF missions. One reality is that the demand is greater. Another reality is that there are numerous places around the globe where civil affairs missions would be appropriate and prudent in order to influence governments and populations, to increase support for friendly governments, and to maintain situational understanding in case contingency operation become required.

In 2009, the 95th Civil Affairs Brigade Commander, Colonel Mike Warmack, implied that as the unit has increased its ability to take on more missions so have the requests from country teams and combatant commands for support. At that time, the brigade had civil affairs elements deployed to over 30 countries. Warmack noted the "Defense Department's growing awareness of the importance of 'soft

---

[100] Sean D. Naylor, "Demand Skyrocketing for Active-Duty Civil Affairs Brigade," *Defense News*, Oct 5, 2009. http://www.defensenews.com/osd_story.php?sh=VSDA&i=3755343, (accessed Nov 20, 2009).

[101] Thomas Hartzel, "TAA 10-15 CA and PSYOP Approved Growth," (briefing, Fort Bragg, NC, 19NOV08), Slide 5.

power'…has led to a growth in resources and responsibility for the…Brigade." One can logically infer from Colonel Warmack's comments is that there is still unmet demand because USASOC and the Army have been building active component civil affairs force structure based on the wrong demand signal. Rather than structuring the active duty civil affairs force based on current mission requests, the Army should adopt a macro level analysis tool on which to base force development decisions.

Macro-level analysis of states' domestic attributes offers to special operations the same proactive and logically structured basis for force development that templated support offers to conventional forces. Use of analyses external to the military removes internal bias. Five existing indexes of state weakness demonstrated potential for determining demand for civil affairs special operations: The Index of Failed States published by the published by the Fund for Peace, the Index of State Weakness published by the Brookings Institute, The State Fragility Index and Matrix published by George Mason University, Human Development Index published by the United Nations Development Program (UNDP), and the Economist Intelligence Unit's Index of Democracy.[102]

The screening criteria used to determine suitability were 1) the index must include a measure of democracy since democracy promotion is a key component of the National Security Strategy; 2) the index must be published every four years or more frequently in order to support the Quadrennial Review process; and 3) the evaluation must consider more than one measurement area. Application of the screening criteria eliminated the UNDP's Human Development Index because it fails to assess democratization and the Economist Intelligence Unit's Index of Democracy because it only directly assesses democratization.[103] Evaluation criteria used to select an index were 1) number of social science

_____

[102] Two other indexes of state fragility were also considered: The World Bank's classification of Low-income Countries Under Stress (LICUS) and the Organization for Economic Cooperation and Development's (OECD) Development Assistance Committee identification of 48 fragile states receiving official development assistance funding.

[103] While the HDI and the EIU's Index of Democracy were eliminated, their assessment of 122 and 137 weak states is consistent with the three indexes that passed screening.

categories assessed to provide as holistic an assessment as possible, where more is better; 2) frequency of publication in order to provide timely notice of changes in the global environment, where more often is better, and 3) independence from government influence to reduce bias and increase legitimacy of the results, where more independent is better.

The Index of Failed States outscored the other two indexes in the unweighted assessment of the evaluation criteria. The Index of Failed States and the Index of State Weakness tied each other with five areas assessed, and outscored the State Fragility Index and Matrix with three areas assessed. In the category of publication frequency, the Index of Failed States scored highest, followed by the Index of State Weakness, followed by the State Fragility Index and Matrix. In the assessment of independence, the State Fragility Index and Matrix scored highest, followed by the Index of Failed States, and then the Index of State Weakness.[104] The following table depicts the evaluation results:

Evaluation criteria	Index of Failed States	Index of State Weakness	State Fragility Index
Assessment areas	1.5	1.5	0
Publication Frequency	2	1	0
Independence	2	1	3
Total	5.5	3.5	3

Figure 2: Evaluation of state macro-level assessment indexes

In addition to the criteria used to assess the indexes, Foreign Policy magazine has been in publication for forty years, lending credibility to the material it publishes.

The Index of Failed States (IFS) published annually by the Fund for Peace in *Foreign Policy* is focused on factors of instability, with the intent to show a particular country's risk of failure. The Fund for Peace has utilized its Conflict Assessment Tool over the past decade to assess states. In 2008, the

---

[104] The educational institution was assessed as most independent, followed by the media, and then the institute which serves clients.

Fund analyzed 177 states.[105] The IFS categorizes 141 countries as other than stable or most stable.[106] The IFS categorizes states in five categories: critical, in danger, borderline, stable, and most stable based on a summation score between zero and one hundred twenty of twelve analysis areas worth zero to ten points each. A lower total score is better, and a score of sixty or greater falls outside the 'stable' categories.[107] Twenty countries are classified 'critical.' Twenty more are classified as 'in danger.' The remaining 101 countries are 'borderline'.[108]

The demand indicated by the Index of Failed States is for Civil Affairs forces in 141 countries or failed states. This analysis will assume that a civil affairs team-alpha (CAT-A), as the smallest whole element in the civil affairs structure, is the appropriate force package to conduct engagement. At the current dwell ratio of 1:1 that active component civil affairs are experiencing, 282 CAT-As are required to maintain persistent engagement; this equates to slightly less than 57 companies, or slightly less than three brigades under the projected five-battalion structure. At a 1:2 dwell ratio, less than the Army objective, but better than the current 1:1 dwell, 423 CAT-As would be required to maintain persistent engagement; this is slightly more than four brigades with five battalions each.

The breakdown of demand by combatant command is conducive to maintaining regional alignment of active component civil affairs units, albeit with a larger structure. CENTCOM is responsible for engagement with twenty countries. In this case, it is prudent to apply a factor of two, resulting in an annual demand for 40 civil affairs teams, or 80 total teams to achieve 1:1 dwell ratio. To achieve a dwell

---

[105] The Fund for Peace, "FAQ & Methodology," *Foreign Policy,* http://www.foreignpolicy.com/articles/ 2009/06/22/2009_failed_states_index_faq_methodology, (accessed Jan 26, 2010)

[106] Fund for Peace, *Foreign Policy,* http://www.foreignpolicy.com/images/ 090624_2009_final_data.pdf, (accessed Jan 26, 2010).

[107] The Fund for Peace, "The Index of Failed States," *Foreign Policy,* http://www.foreignpolicy.com/ articles/2009/06/22/2009_failed_states_index_interactive_map_and_rankings, (accessed Jan 26, 2010). The twelve indicators are demographic pressures, refugees/IDPs, group grievance, human flight, uneven development, economic decline, delegitimization of the state, public services, human rights, security apparatus, factionalized elites, and external intervention.

[108] http://www.foreignpolicy.com/images/090624_2009_final_data.pdf. Accessed January 26, 2010.

ratio would require 120 teams, equivalent to a six-battalion brigade. PACOM conducts engagement with 36 countries. 72 civil affairs teams would be required to achieve 1:1 dwell ratio. 108 teams would be required to achieve a 1:2 dwell ratio, roughly equivalent to a five-battalion brigade. AFRICOM engages 53 countries, requiring 106 teams to achieve 1:1 dwell. A brigade of approximately eight battalions or two brigades of four battalions are required to achieve 1:2 dwell ratio. SOUTHCOM conduct engagement with 32 countries, which would require 64 teams to achieve 1:1 dwell time. Achieving 1:2 dwell time requires 96 teams, equivalent to a five-battalion brigade. EUCOM and NORTHCOM demand could be met by a four-battalion brigade.

Civil Affairs Force Structure

<u>Special Operations Truths</u>
Humans are more important than hardware
SOF cannot be mass produced
Quality is better than quantity
Competent SOF cannot be created after emergencies occur
Most Special Operations require non-SOF support[109]

The inability of the current civil affairs force structure to meet contemporary demands stems from decisions made by Army leaders in the wake of the Vietnam War and perpetuated even today. In 1974, Creighton Abrams moved the majority of supporting forces into the Reserves, including most civil affairs units. The movement of forces to the reserves was both politically and fiscally motivated. Movement of most of the support capability into the Army Reserve was intended to prevent another commitment of U.S. Army forces to a sustained conflict without Congressional declaration of war, supported by the citizenry. Furthermore, in the years after the Vietnam War, the Administration and Congress were cutting the defense budget; placing support units in the Reserve was a cost cutting measure to maintain the fighting proficiency of maneuver units. As a result, the bulk of the civil affairs units were placed in the Army Reserve; one battalion was retained in the active force to support special operations and provide immediate support for contingency missions.[110] As the global environment has changed since the end of the Cold War, invalidating the assumptions that led to placement of civil affairs units in the Reserves, the Army has reactively initiated inadequate growth in force structure to meet increasing demand for civil affairs. The next four sections will address reserve component force structure changes from 1989 to 2010, active component growth since the end of the Cold War, approved force structure changes for 2011 to 2015, and force structure changes currently under consideration in the 2010 Quadrennial Review.

---

[109] USSOCOM, *Fact Book: United States Special Operations Command*, (Tampa, FL: USSOCOM, 2010) 44-45. http://www.socom.mil/SOCOMHome/newspub/pubs/Documents/FactBook.pdf, (accessed 22Mar10).

[110] Lawrence J. Kolb, "Fixing the Mix," *Foreign Affairs* 83, no. 2 (March 2004), 2.

Reserve Component Structure and Capabilities

Although operational tempo increased for Civil Affairs in the 1990s as conflict shifted from traditional interstate conflict to more irregular warfare, including nation-building efforts in Kuwait, Somalia, Haiti, Bosnia, and Kosovo, Civil Affairs force structure remained fairly static throughout the decade. In the early 1990s civil affairs groups were redesignated brigades. In the 1993 *Civil Affairs Operations* field manual, the Army designated civil affairs battalions as 'foreign internal defense/unconventional warfare' (FID/UW) in support of special operations, direct support (DS) of European Command (EUCOM), and general purpose (GP).[111] In 1999, the 361st Civil Affairs Brigade was redesignated as the 350th Civil Affairs Command, bringing the total number of CACOMs to four and aligning one with each combatant command outside the continental United States.[112] The lack of significant changes in the civil affairs force structure during the 1990s is indicative of the fact that it was able to meet operational demand. Those conditions changed when the United States initiated the Global War on Terror, and by 2004 leaders were beginning to recognize that some growth and restructuring of Civil Affairs was necessary to meet increased demand from irregular warfare and nation-building. In 2005, the Army restructured Civil Affairs as part of Force Design Update (FDU) 05-01.

Force Design Update 05-01 was the result of series of six memos from Secretary of Defense Donald Rumsfeld called 'snowflakes' that questioned whether Civil Affairs should continue to be designated special operations forces, and indicated that they should be transferred to a conventional command. Although every command impacted by the proposed change was opposed to it, General Schoomaker ultimately published General Order No. 12 effective October 1, 2006, that transferred the USACAPOC from the USASOC to U.S. Army reserve Command (USARC). On November 14, 2006, Deputy Secretary of Defense Gordon England directed the transfer of USACAPOC and rescinded their

---

[111] Field Manual 41-10, 1993, 4-1.

[112] Global Security, "350th Civil Affairs Command," under "Military," http://www.globalsecurity.org/military/agency/army/350ca-cmd.htm, (accessed 21Mar10).

designation as special operations forces.[113] FDU 05-01 initiated three major changes in the reserve component civil affairs force structure. First, it authorized reserve civil affairs expansion from 6,268 to 7,152 personnel and the activation of four new battalions for a new total of 28. Second, it authorized the addition of tactical CA companies in each reserve component battalion to align the battalions' structure to support modular brigade combat teams. Finally, it transferred USACAPOC and all reserve component civil affairs units to the USARC.[114]

The current reserve component civil affairs structure, under the command and control of the U.S. Army Civil Affairs and Psychological Operations Command, consists of four Civil Affairs commands (CACOM), eight Civil Affairs brigades, twenty-eight Civil Affairs battalions, and 112 Civil Affairs companies. The CACOM is designed to provide support to a theater ground combat commander or field army commander. Four CACOMs offer the ability to provide persistent support to a field Army. However, since the end of the Cold War, only during the two invasions of Iraq has the United States fielded a force approximating field army size, and then for no more than a year. USASOC noted in their analysis that a portion of a CACOM has been deployed in support of Operations Iraqi Freedom and Enduring Freedom, but that a CACOM has not recently deployed as a whole unit. The civil affairs brigade deploys to support a corps headquarters. Eight brigades provide the ability to support two corps simultaneously in enduring operations at an operational tempo of 1:2 based on nine months 'boots on the ground.' The 28 battalions that support division headquarters can support the average six deployed division headquarters continuously at an operational tempo of 1:3.5 given the current 'boots on the ground' limitation. USASOC noted in 2008 that only two civil affairs battalion headquarters were deploying at a time to support Operations Iraqi Freedom and Enduring Freedom. [115] The current 112 Civil

---

[113] Hugh C. VanRoosen, "Implications of the 2006 Reassignment of U.S. Army Civil Affairs," (Carlisle Barracks, PA: U.S. Army War College, 2009), 4-9.

[114] Castellanos, 3.

[115] Hartzel, "CA Force Structure Analysis," Slide 9.

Affairs companies are operating at a 1:2.2 dwell in order to support the maneuver brigades, provincial reconstruction teams, and human terrain teams in the two theaters of operations.[116] However, the organizational structure of reserve civil affairs only tells part of the story; accounting for the U.S. Army Reserve's ability to man these units to full strength significantly changes capabilities.

In addition to the structural shortfalls to support twenty brigades in enduring operations, reserve civil affairs units are facing recruiting and retention problems, often linked to short dwell times, resulting in a 85% or less fill of civil affairs duty positions.[117] Of the positions that are filled, only 86% of the soldiers have completed training and are qualified for duty. The 2008 USASOC assessment noted that the USAR can only source 9.6 companies annually at a 1:4 operational tempo with nine months 'boots on the ground'.[118] Reserve civil affairs units are 'robbing Peter to pay Paul' buy using volunteers and new soldiers assigned to other units to fill deploying units.

USACAPOC also faces challenges resourcing reserve component battalions and brigades, the holding units for functional specialists and planning teams. "Civil affairs commands provide expertise in six functional specialty areas: rule of law, economic stability, governance, public health and welfare, infrastructure, and public education and information. USAR CA brigades and battalions have capabilities in four of the functional specialty areas: rule of law, governance, health and welfare, and infrastructure."[119] Unlike active civil affairs units, reserve units are not regionally aligned, but instead bring subject matter expertise from their civilian employment. This is significant because functional specialists are capability that does not currently exist in the active component civil affairs brigade and is needed to support both conventional and special operations.[120] Functional specialty capabilities residing

---

[116] Ibid., Slide 6. The Army made a fiscal decision to resource only 112 CA Companies instead of the 120 directed by FDU 05-01.

[117] Castellanos, 3-4.

[118] Hartzel, "CA Force Structure Analysis," Slide 5.

[119] FM 3-05.40, 2006, 1-9.

[120] Ibid.

in the reserve component, designated as conventional forces, and supporting both conventional and special operations is one symptom of the command, control, and proponency issues generated by the transition of USACAPOC from USASOC to USARC.

Transfer of the reserve Civil Affairs forces from USASOC to the USARC has complicated command, control, and coordination of Army Civil Affairs to achieve unity of effort in overseas contingency operations and special operations. The current force structure requires the coordination of four four-star headquarters – combatant command, Joint Forces Command, Forces Command, and Special Operations Command – as well as two three-star headquarters, USACAPOC, and the 95th Civil Affairs Brigade to resource all the civil affairs forces required in combat theaters.

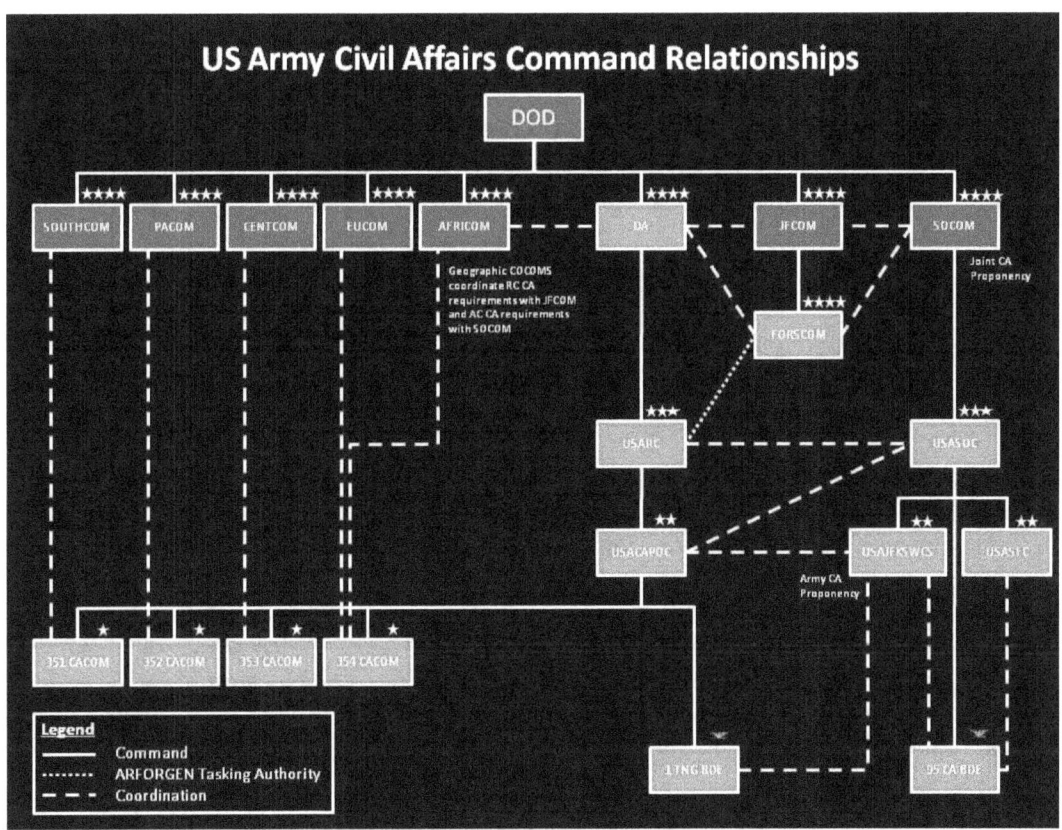

Figure 3: US Army Civil Affairs command relationships after USACAPOC transfer to USARC[121]

---

[121] Adaptation of original USACAPOC presentation slide to depict only civil affairs units, highlight Civil Affairs proponency, and add command rank structure.

The structure also complicates the process for resourcing reserve component functional specialists to support special operations after the 95th CA Brigade's generalist complete assessments and apply initial short-term remedial actions. In the current system, the U.S Special Forces Command, or the U.S. Army Special Operations Command must generate a request for forces (RFF) through U.S. Special Operations Command to Joint Forces Command (JFCOM). JFCOM, in turn generates a tasking through Forces Command (FORSCOM) and U.S. Army Reserve Command to USACAPOC. These requirements are in addition to conventional force requirements generated in the Army Force Generation (ARFORGEN) process. The structure complicates the coordination and synchronization of deployed civil affairs forces in a theater of operation because reporting chains run through different headquarters and do not merge until the four-star joint level.

Active Component Capabilities and Structure

Unlike the reserve component mix of civil affairs generalists and functional specialists, the active component is composed strictly of civil affairs generalists. Active duty civil affairs soldiers are linguists and culturally attuned to their area of operations, but are "generalists trained 'to map the civil human terrain and then identify the civil vulnerabilities that can be exploited' by terrorists and insurgents in developing nations."[122] Doctrinally, the purpose of active component civil affairs remains to provide initial assessment and immediate remedial actions until reserve component civil affairs forces can mobilize to support special operations and conventional forces. The reality is that active component civil affairs are providing long-term support to country teams and combatant commands around the globe in places such as the Philippines, Colombia, and the Horn of Africa, without functional expertise.

From 1989 to 2004, there were very few, and mostly minor, modifications to the active component civil affairs structure. Most changes were internal restructuring of the one active component

---

[122] Naylor, "Demand Skyrocketing for Active-Duty Civil Affairs Brigade," Oct 5, 2009. http://www.defensenews.com/osd_story.php?sh=VSDA&i=3755343. Accessed Nov 20, 2009.

battalion, the 96th Civil Affairs Battalion, in order to better meet increasing demand. Until 2005, there was little interest outside the battalion to increase the force structure. However, as the wars in Iraq and Afghanistan dragged on, and it became obvious that growth was necessary to supporting the persistent operations of Enduring Freedom and other special operations around the globe. Prior to 2006, civil affairs doctrinal support for special operations was a civil affairs company, composed of five civil affairs teams-alpha (CAT-A), aligned with a combatant command and a special forces group, composed of 54 special forces operational detachments-alpha (SFODAs). Special forces ODAs and civil affairs CAT-As generally deploy on a dwell ratio of 1:1. Due in large part to the dispersed nature of special operations throughout the combatant commands, civil affairs elements could only co-locate and provide support to one-sixth of the special forces groups' ODAs, assuming that the Civil Affairs battalion was not tasked for separate missions.

The 2005 Force Design Update 05-01 resulted in two significant changes in the active component civil affairs force. First, it authorized active component civil affairs growth from 409 to 884 personnel and activation of the 95th Civil Affairs Brigade with four battalions. The 95th Civil Affairs Brigade (Airborne) was activated in August 2006 at Fort Bragg, North Carolina. The 95th already has three battalions at full strength and is currently fleshing out a fourth battalion, which will provide commanders the capability to deploy 40 civil affairs teams at a 1:1 dwell ratio, as well as civil affairs planning teams, and civil military operation centers in support of ambassadors and combatant commanders.

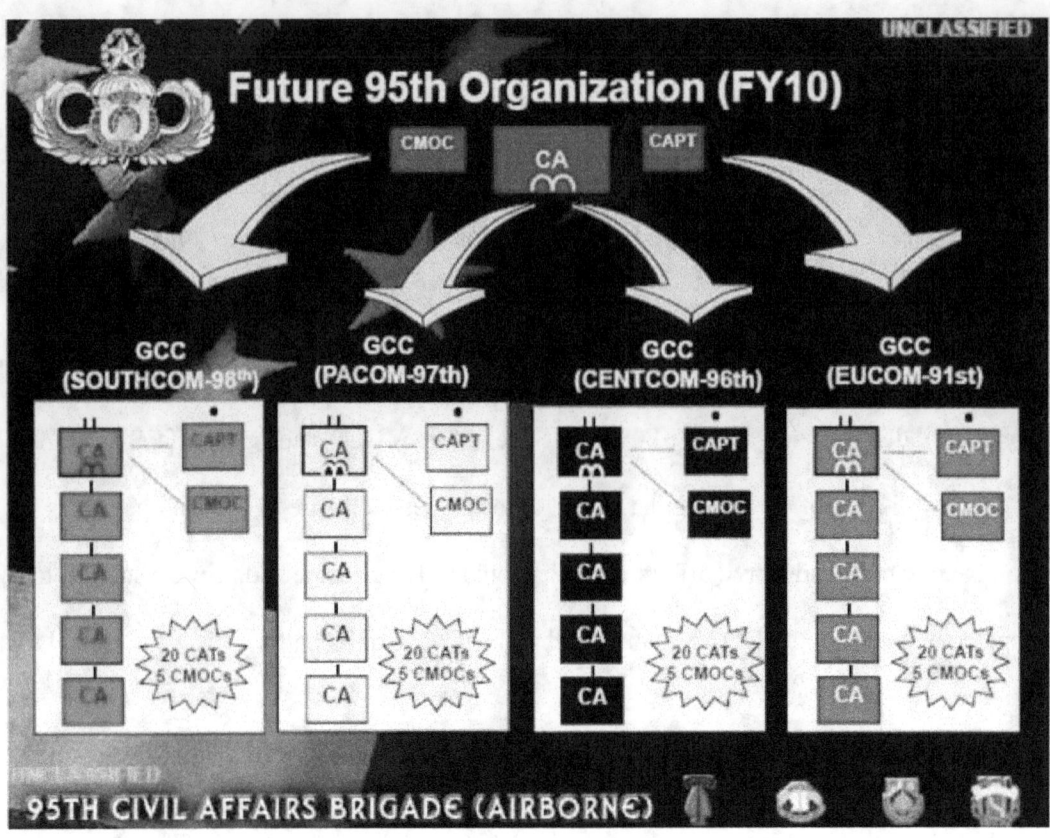

Figure 4: Active component civil affairs structure (FY 2010)[123]

A planned fifth battalion, the result of activation of AFRICOM as a separate geographic combatant command, is intended to allow the brigade to align a battalion in support of each unified combatant command outside the continental United States. [124] The second change, the transfer of USACAPOC from USASOC to USARC, resulted in the 95th CA Brigade becoming a direct reporting unit to USASOC, a three-star headquarters. [125] While this change likely has had significant impact on organizational dynamics, it has little impact on the force structure or the unit's capabilities.

---

[123] Ferdinand Irrizary, "95th Civil Affairs Brigade (Airborne)," command briefing.

[124] Naylor, "Demand Skyrocketing for Active-Duty Civil Affairs Brigade."

[125] Castellanos, 3.

Approved Growth 2010 to 2015

The Total Army Analysis for fiscal years 2010-2015, approved the addition of one battalion and nine additional companies to the current structure of the 95th Civil Affairs Brigade, as well as the activation of a new brigade with five battalions to support conventional forces. Six options were considered for how to utilize the approve growth in personnel end strength, including assigning a civil affairs company to each brigade combat team, growth of two CA brigades in USASOC, several options involving reserve component structure, and the chosen option to create a brigade to support general purpose forces.[126] The additional battalion will allow the 95th CA Brigade to maintain 50 civil affairs teams deployed at a 1:1 dwell ratio. At a 1:2 dwell ratio, the brigade can maintain 33 teams deployed. The U.S. Army authorized the growth and activation of the 85th Civil Affairs Brigade at Fort Hood with five battalions and 30 companies, beginning in fiscal year 2011. If the growth mirrors the previous expansion by the 95th Civil Affairs Brigade of a battalion each fiscal year, the brigade will achieve full operating strength in fiscal 2015. The brigade is intended to support conventional forces. Once the brigade achieves full strength, its ability to deploy at the objective dwell ratio of 1:2 will reduce reserve component demand by 30 companies annually to 210. The capabilities of the brigade will reduce the demand for civil affairs generalist support from the reserve component both in theaters of war and in support of the combatant commands' theater security cooperation plans. As currently envisioned, it will not be used to meet demand for special operations, although the ability to shift the brigade's assets to special operations exists.

---

[126] Hartzel, "TAA 10-15 CA and PSYOP Approved Growth," Slide 7.

Recommendations and Conclusion

The most likely situation where U.S. national interests are at stake will occur in situations short of war. Operations short of war, which include peacetime engagement, demand a new proactive planning focus to promote regional stability as a means to deter conflict. By helping [host nations] provide for their own defense needs and develop sustainable responsive institutions, the Army may reduce the likelihood that it will have to deploy to protect threatened U.S. interests. These operations will emphasize the indirect use of forces in roles that support other nations in their efforts to maintain stability, law, and order.[127]

The foregoing analysis leads directly to three recommendations. First, restructure the reserve component civil affairs force design to create additional companies and eliminate excess higher level headquarters, especially CACOMs. Second, grow the active component civil affairs force to six brigades in order to conduct persistent engagement in support of combatant commanders' accomplishment of national strategic objectives. Finally, place all Army civil affairs forces under the command of a single headquarters reporting through USASOC to USSOCOM, the joint proponent for civil affairs.

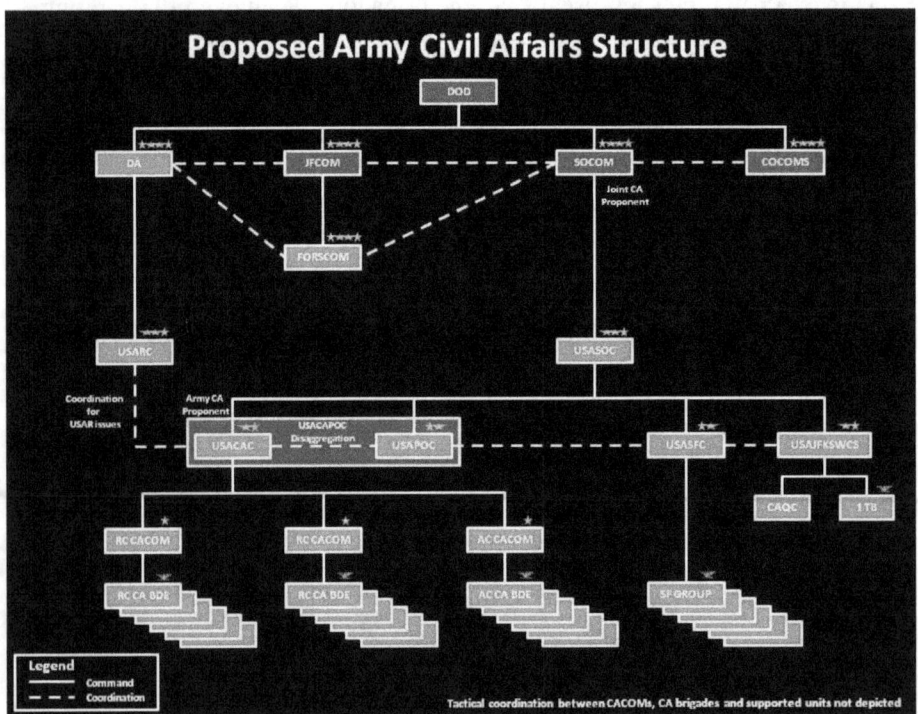

Figure 5: Proposed Army Civil Affairs force structure

---

[127] Field Manual 41-10, (1993), 8-1.

Restructure Reserve Component Civil Affairs

The Army Reserve civil affairs force structure is inadequate to support two corps in enduring operations. Reserve component units are filling deploying units with volunteers from other units that have recently returned from Iraq or Afghanistan and frequently have less than 1:4 dwell time. The strain on the reserves is impacting soldier morale, family support, and employer support; recruiting and retention for civil affairs is dropping. The Department of Defense and the Army are making up shortfalls with 'in lieu of' assignments of shake-and-bake civil affairs officers and noncommissioned officers run through the civil affairs qualification course.[128] These graduates, including mid-level officers, are learning on the job and lack the wisdom that comes from experience and mentoring by seasoned leaders. The result is that although brigade commanders frequently have great soldiers working tirelessly to support the brigade, they do not receive organized units with seasoned operators that can draw on experience to produce exceptional results.[129]

Unless the Army expands and restructures Reserve civil affairs forces, the end state for authorized growth will support 16.8 company equivalents annually, 4.8 battalion headquarters annually, and 1.3 brigade headquarters annually. The United States Army should expand restructure the reserve component civil affairs force structure to support two corps, with six division headquarters, and twenty brigades in simultaneous, enduring regional operations at a 1:5 dwell ratio. Assuming that the total mobilization limitation of one year will not be lifted, the force should be grown by 48 companies, 20 battalion headquarters, and eight brigade headquarters, yielding 160 companies, 48 battalion headquarters, and 16 brigade headquarters. This does not account for micro-environmental demand to support provincial reconstruction teams, human terrain teams, and other Enduring Freedom requirements; this demand adds an additional 60 company requirement.

---

[128] Castellanos, 3-5.

[129] Conversation with 1st Cavalry Division G9 Civil Military Operations Officer in Baghdad in January 2008.

Recent history indicates that four civil affairs commands are not needed. Operations by theater armies are generally one year or less in duration. While the retained CACOMs must be deployable, they would primarily function as force providers, manning, equipping and training Civil Affairs units for deployment. The recommendation is to deactivate two reserve component CACOMS and transfer the personnel to other units to improve unit strengths. Each of the two CACOMs, commanded by a brigadier general, should have seven to eight Civil Affairs brigades, each composed of three battalions, to allow for a 1:5 dwell ratio. The reserve component would primarily serve during conflict and post-conflict, as the reserve system is intended to function. Outside of traditional warfare and post-conflict reconstruction, the reserve forces would support combatant command and Army service component command (ASCC) theater security cooperation plans and humanitarian actions during annual training and short-term mobilization.

Grow Active Component Civil Affairs

The approved end state for growth of active component civil affairs units to two brigades, with one conducting special operations and one supporting conventional forces, is both insufficient and allocates active component manpower against a reserve component requirement. The 95th Civil Affairs Brigade is currently only able to meet approximately one-third of the micro-level environmental demand. Were the planned 85th Civil Affairs Brigade allocated against special operations, it would still not meet current demand. However, the macro-level environmental demand is significantly greater. In order to maintain persistent engagement in the 141 countries at a 1:2 dwell ratio requires 423 civil affairs teams, or approximately 85 civil affairs companies. The growth required beyond that which has already been approved is 45 companies. Maintaining the status quo 1:1 dwell ratio requires 282 teams, or approximately 57 companies.

The active component of the Civil Affairs branch should be grown to six brigades. The brigades would be primarily responsible for supporting the combatant commands' theater special operations command requirements. CENTCOM, responsible for engagement in 20 countries, should be allocated a brigade consisting of four battalions (applies a factor of two to account for national security interests in the region and ongoing conflict). PACOM, responsible for cooperation with 36 countries should be allocated a brigade consisting of four battalions. AFRICOM, which interacts with 53 countries, including the Trans-Sahara countries should be allocated two brigades of four battalions. SOUTHCOM, responsible for engagement with 32 countries should be allocated a brigade of four battalions. A final brigade of four battalions should provide forces for EUCOM and NORTHCOM; these two regions consist of primarily of OECD countries. This force structure will permit persistent engagement in virtually every country in the geographic combatant commands with a dwell ratio of 1:2 for active forces. An implication of the forgoing increase in force structure is the need for a headquarters to command and control the six brigades. The Army should establish a one-star, active component civil affairs command. While the headquarters, or a detachment, should be deployable, it would primarily serve as a force provider.

Restructure Army Civil Affairs Command and Control

When Secretary of Defense Rumsfeld instigated the transfer of reserve component civil affairs out of the special operations community, he significantly complicated the command and control of civil affairs units. It appears that he did not distinguish between special operations forces integration with conventional forces and conversion of civil affairs to conventional forces. The 'divorce' of active duty and reserve component civil affairs, as some authors have referred to the transfer of USACAPOC to USARC, is like one with children. Although the reserve component, and its headquarters, are no longer in the special operations family, USACAPOC is still expected to support special operations with functional specialists, skills that do not exist in the active duty force structure.[130] However, if one looks at the specialized training that civil affairs operators receive, both in and out of the military, combined with their

---

[130] Hugh C. VanRoosen, "Implications of the 2006 Reassignment of U.S. Army Civil Affairs," (Carlisle Barracks, PA: U.S. Army War College, 2009), 1-4.

mode of operation in small teams, often in low profile missions, civil affairs clearly meets the definition

of SOF:

> Army Special Operations Forces (ARSOF) are specially organized, trained, and equipped
> military forces. They conduct [special operations] to achieve military, political,
> economic, or informational objectives by generally unconventional means in hostile,
> denied, or politically sensitive areas...ARSOF operations differ from conventional
> operations by their degree of acceptable physical and political risk, their modes of
> employment, and their operational techniques.[131]

It appears that Secretary Rumsfeld had a very short-sighted perspective of civil affairs, seeing them only

as battlefield forces in Afghanistan and Iraq, and ignoring all the special operations that civil affairs were

conducting around the globe. This mistake needs to be fixed, restoring the special operations status of all

civil affairs and reintegrating all civil affairs forces under one command.

U.S. Army Civil Affairs and Psychological Operations Command, as it currently exists, should be

transferred back to the active component under USASOC. It should then be disaggregated into the U.S.

Army Civil Affairs Command and the U.S. Army Psychological Operations Command, each under the

command of a major general, irrespective of component, who also serves as the chief of the respective

branches. Although an active duty command once again, it should be a blended organization of active and

reserve duty positions.

Conclusion

When the United States Army leadership transitioned Civil Affairs, along with many other

combat support units, to the Army Reserves, it did not envision a world of persistent engagement. The

Global War on Terror was a wake-up call that the United States needed to take action to counter and then

pre-empt non-state actors' challenge of the international rule set. The United States must improve it use of

smart power. Although the U.S. is extremely proficient in the application of hard power, we must increase

---

[131] Department of the Army, *Field Manual 3-05: Army Special Operations Forces*, Washington, D.C.:
GPO, 2006), 1-11.

our capacity and the capabilities for application of soft power. The Department of Defense must expand and develop the resources to employ soft power because there are many environments where it is morally irresponsible to expect unarmed civilians to operate, or to arm civilians, making them un-uniformed combatants. Even in more permissive environments, the DOD should partner with other interagency efforts both to enhance their capabilities, as well as to develop civil information to prepare for the possibilities of conventional, special, or humanitarian operations.

Civil Affairs, often called 'social workers with guns,' are a key component of a whole-of-government approach to fostering stability, especially in hostile or semi-permissive regions. Civil Affairs units have the ability to assess conditions, perform immediate remedial actions, and then follow up with long term solutions that reduce factors of instability in partnership with interagency, intergovernmental, and nongovernmental partners. Civil Affairs soldiers are, however, a very limited asset. Expansion of active and reserve civil affairs force structure is essential as a component of the whole-of-government approach and to reduce the necessity to deploy lethal combat power to protect U.S interests. The major take-away from a 2007 Civil Affairs Association roundtable was the recommendations that "the U.S. Army [should] base the size of its Civil Affairs for on the projected Joint and national security requirements in addition to supporting U.S. Army units."[132] Restructuring Civil Affairs force structure as described in this monograph will align one of the critical military means of applying soft power with the ways and means outlined in national strategy documents.

---

[132] The Civil Affairs Association, "Civil Affairs Force Structure," Issue Paper #1. November 2007. http://www.CivilAffairsassoc.org/CAA%20Issue%20Papers%20Nov%2007.pdf.

APPENDIX A: Glossary

AC – Active Component

ARFORGEN – Army Force Generation

ASCC – Army Service Component Command

BCT – Brigade Combat Team

CA – Civil Affairs

CACOM – Civil Affairs Command

CAO – Civil Affairs Operations

CAPT – Civil Affairs Planning Team

CAT-A – Civil Affairs Team-Alpha

CD – Civil Defense

CIM – Civil Information Management

CLT – Civil Liaison Team

CMO – Civil-Military Operations

CMOC – Civil Military Operations Cell

CMSE – Civil Military Support Element

DOD – Department of Defense

DODI – Department of Defense Instruction

DOS – Department of State

DS – Direct Support

Dwell time – The amount of time spent at home station between deployments

Dwell ratio – The amount of time deployed (d) compared to the amount of time home (h), d:h

FID – Foreign Internal Defense

FDU – Force Design Update

FHA – Foreign Humanitarian Assistance

FM – Field Manual

FNS – Foreign Nation Support

GP – General Purpose

HA – Humanitarian Assistance

HASC – House Arms Services Committee

HDI – Human Development Index

IFS – Index of Failed States

ISW – Index of State Weakness

IW – Irregular Warfare

JOC – Joint Operating Concept

JP – Joint Publication

MCA – Military Civic Action

MMAS – Masters of Military Arts and Science (granted by CGSC)

NA – Nation Assistance

NDS – National Defense Strategy

NMS – National Military Strategy

NSS – National Security Strategy

PRC – Population and Resources Control

QDR – Quadrennial Defense Review

RC – Reserve Component

SCA – Support to Civil Administration

S/CRS – State Coordinator for Reconstruction and Stabilization

SF – Special Forces

SFODA – Special Force Operation Detachment-Alpha (A-Team)

SO – Special Operations

SOF – Special Operations Forces

SSTR – Stability, Security, Transition, and Reconstruction

TAA – Total Army Analysis

TSCP – Theater Security Cooperation Plan

UNDP – United Nations Development Program

USARC - United States Army Reserve Command

USACAC – U.S. Army Civil Affairs Command (proposed); U.S. Army Combined Arms Center (propose renaming to U.S. Army Institute of Land Warfare)

USACAPOC – U.S. Army Civil Affairs and Psychological Operations Command

USAID – United States Agency for International Development

USAJFKSWCS – U.S. Army John F. Kennedy Special Warfare Center and School

USAPOC – United States Army Psychological Operations Command (proposed)

USASOC – United States Army Special Operations Command

USCENTCOM – United States Central Command (also CENTCOM)

USEUCOM – United States European Command (also EUCOM)

USNORTHCOM – United States Northern Command (also NORTHCOM)

USPACOM – United States Pacific Command (also PACOM)

USSOUTHCOM – United States Southern Command (also SOUTHCOM)

USSOCOM-U.S. Special Operations Command

UW – Unconventional Warfare

APPENDIX B: Reserve Component CA Force Structure (2010)

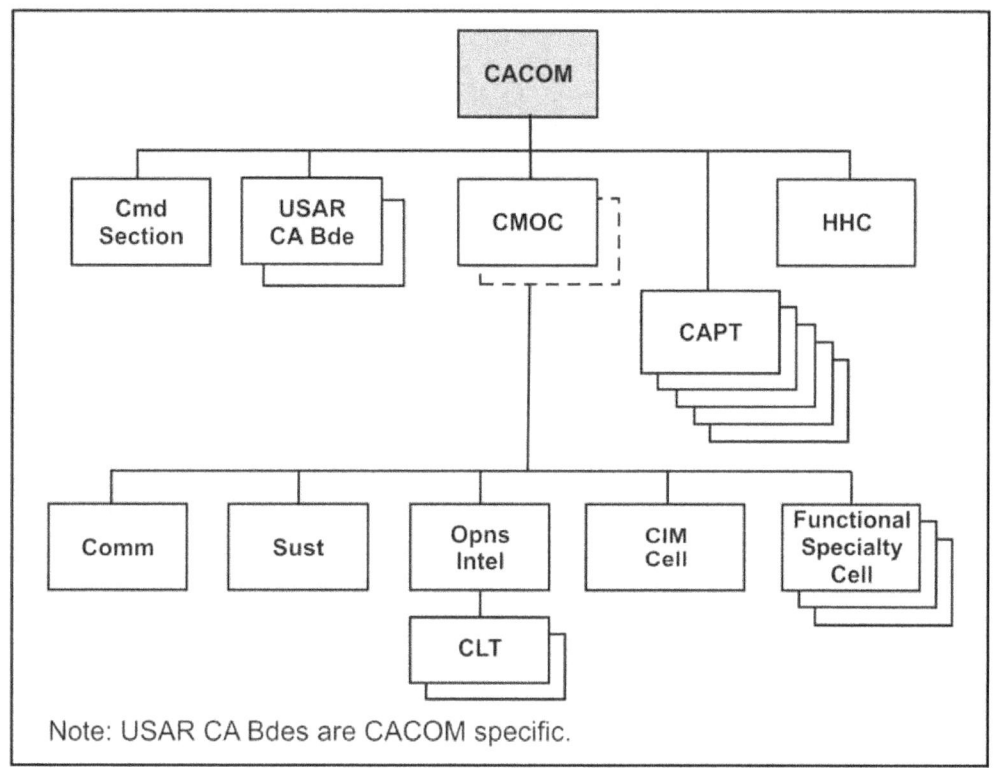

Figure 6: Reserve component CA command structure (FM 3-05.40, 2006)

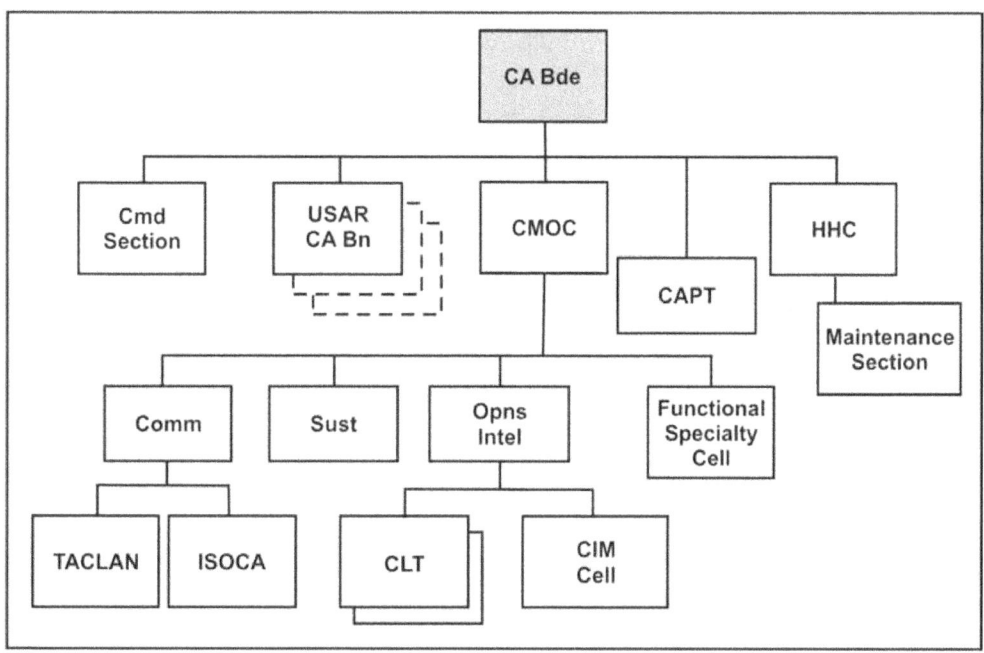

Figure 7: Reserve component CA brigade structure (FM 3-05.40, 2006)

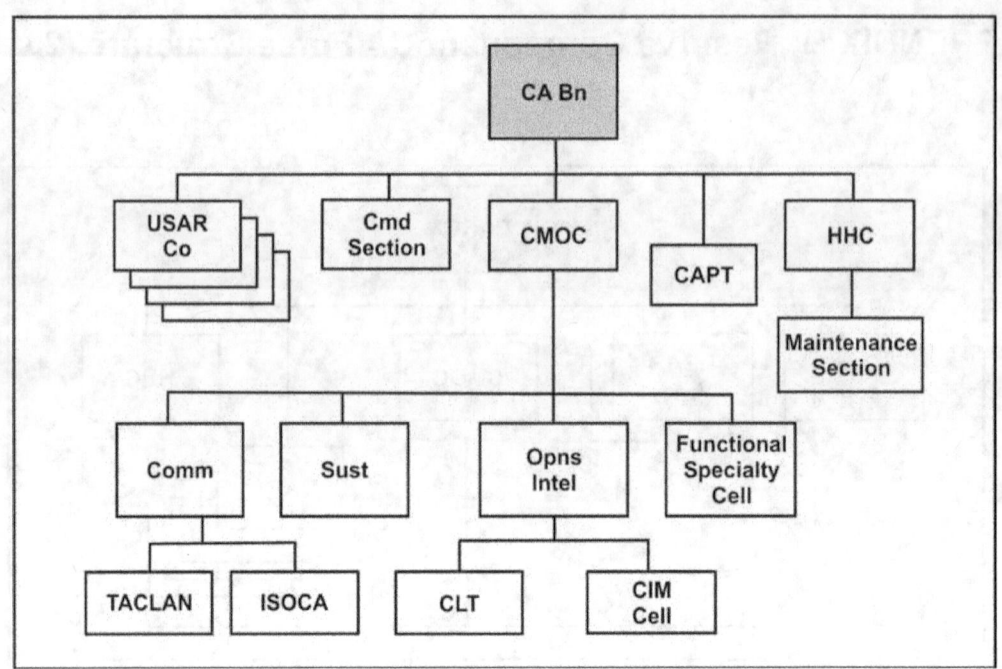

Figure 8: Reserve component CA battalion structure (FM 3-05.40, 2006)

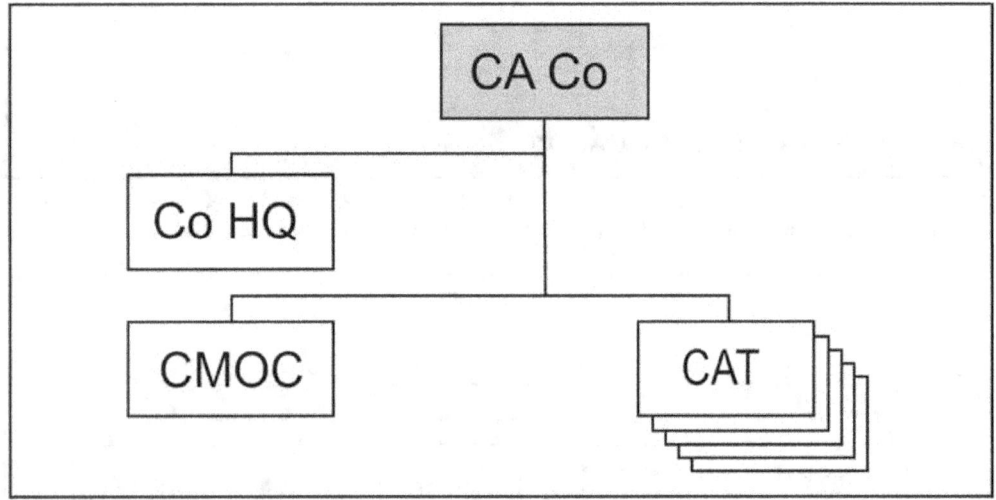

Figure 9: Reserve and component CA company structure (FM 3-05.40, 2006)

APPENDIX C: Active Component CA Force Structure (2010)

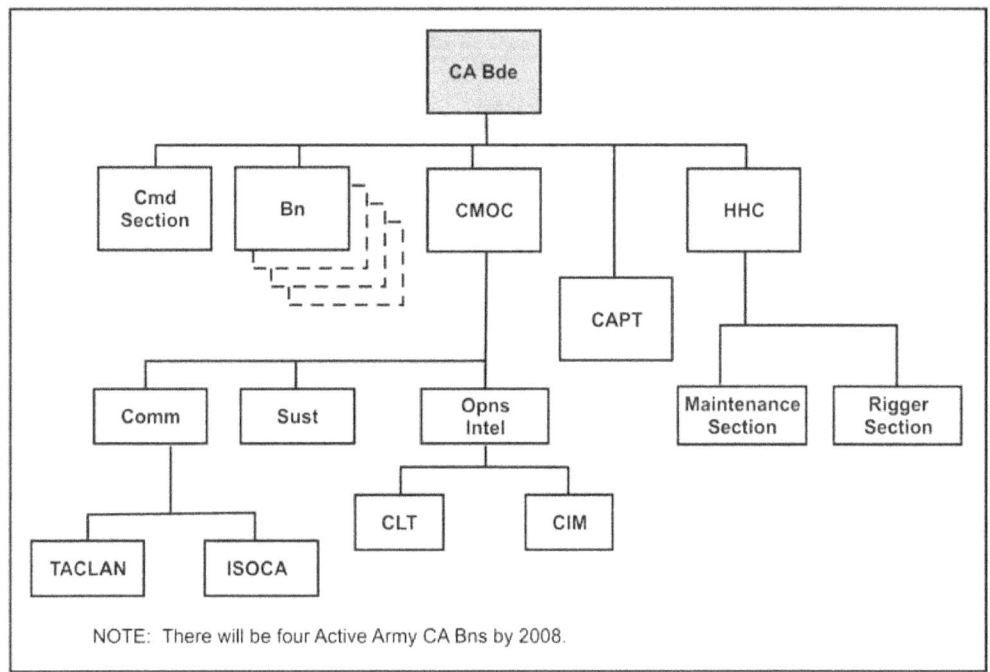

Figure 10: Active component CA brigade structure (FM 3-05.40, 2006)

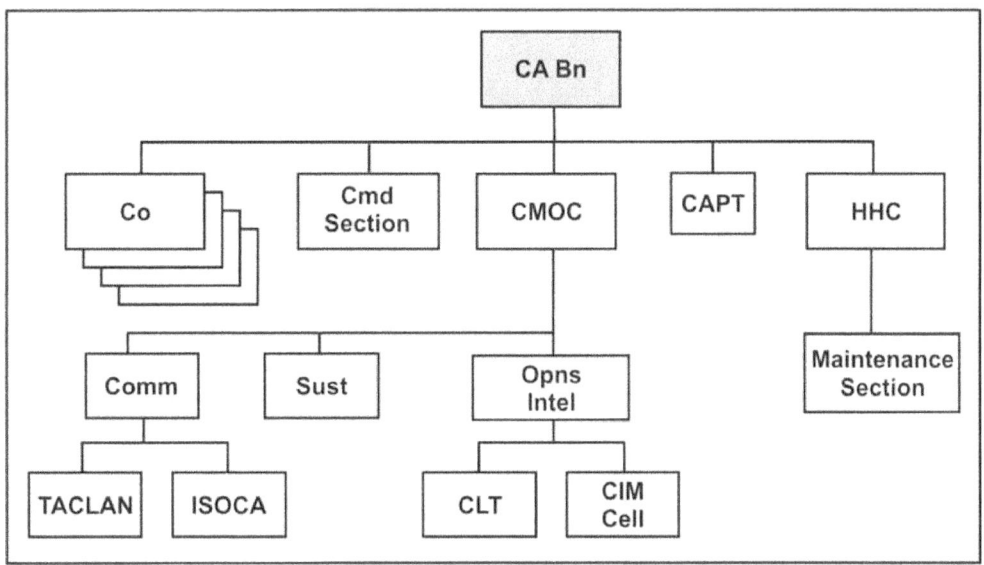

Figure 11: Active component CA battalion structure (FM 3-05.40, 2006)

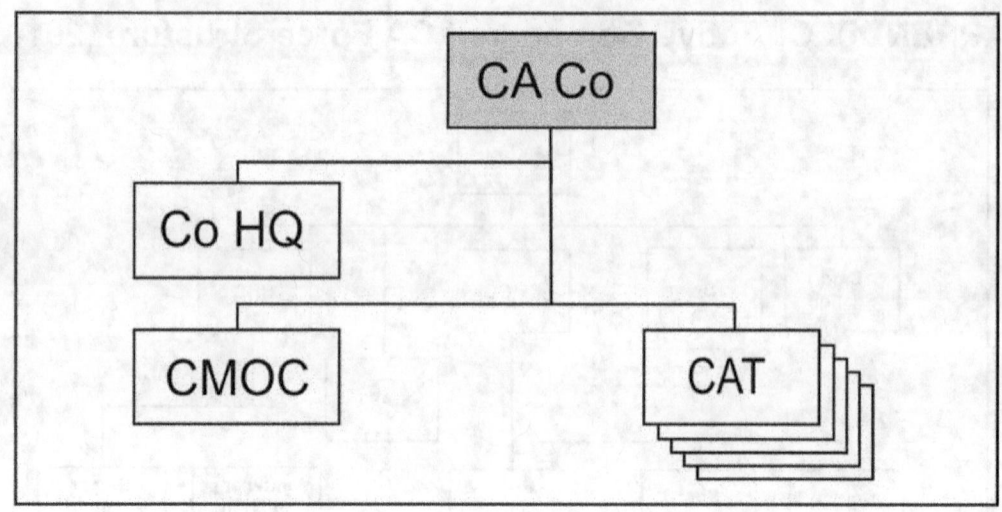

Figure 12: Reserve and Active Component CA Company structure (FM 3-05.40, 2006)

BIBLIOGRAPHY

Assistant Secretary of Defense for Special Operations, Low Intensity Conflict & Interdependent Capabilities. "Report to Congress on Civil Affairs." Washington, DC: Department of Defense, 2009.

Barnett, Thomas P. M. *Blueprint for Action: A Future Worth Creating*. New York: Berkley Books, 2005.

---. *The Pentagon's New Map*. New York: Berkley Books, 2004.

Bingham, Bruce B. Daniel L. Rubini and Michael J. Cleary. "U.S. Army Civil Affairs: The Army's 'Ounce of Prevention.'" Arlington, Va.: Institute of Land Warfare, Association of the United States Army, 2003.

Brewer, R.C. "U.S. Army Civil Affairs and the Fate of Reserve Special Operations Forces in Support of Current and Future Operations." Ft. Belvoir: Defense Technical Information Center, 2004. http://www.dtic.mil/cgi-bin/GetTRDoc?AD=ADA423315&Location=U2&doc=GetTRDoc.pdf.

Castellanos, Miguel A. "Civil Affairs – Building the Force to Meet Its Future Challenges," Carlisle Barracks, PA: U.S. Army War College, 2009.

Chairman Joint Chiefs of Staff. *CJCSM 3113.01: Theater Engagement Planning*. Washington, D.C.: Joint Staff, 1998.

Collier, Paul, Anke Hoeffler, and Nicholas Sambanis. "The Collier-Hoeffler Model of Civil War Onset and the Case Study Project Research Design." *Understanding Civil War*. Vol 2. Ed. Paul Collier and Nicholas Sambanis. Washington, D.C.: The World Bank, 2005.

Department of Defense. Briefing. "Quadrennial Defense Review and Ballistic Missile Defense Review." (February 1, 2010) http://www.defense.gov/news/d2010usdprolloutbrief.pdf, (Accessed March 27, 2010).

---. "Department of Defense Directive 3000.05: Military Support for Stability, Security, transition, and Reconstruction Operations." Washington, D.C: Department of Defense, 2005.

---. "Department of Defense Directive 3000.05: Military Support for Stability, Security, transition, and Reconstruction Operations." Washington, D.C: Department of Defense, 2009.

---. *National Defense Strategy*. Washington, DC: Department of Defense, 2008. http://purl.access.gpo.gov/GPO/LPS103291

---. *National Defense Strategy of the United States of America*. Washington, DC: Department of Defense, 2008. http://purl.access.gpo.gov/GPO/LPS59037

---. *Quadrennial Defense Review Report*. Washington, D.C.: Department of Defense, 2001.

---. *Quadrennial Defense Review Report*. Washington, D.C.: Department of Defense, 2006.

---. *Quadrennial Defense Review Report*. Washington, D.C.: Department of Defense, 2010.

---. *Report on the Bottom-Up Review*. Washington, D.C.: Department of Defense, 1993.

---. "Report to Congress on Civil Affairs." Washington, D.C.: GPO, 2009.

Department of the Army. *Field Manual 3-05: Army Special Operations Forces*, Washington, D.C.: GPO, 2006.

---. *Field Manual 3-05.40: Civil Affairs Operations*. Washington, DC: GPO, 2006.

---. *Field Manual 41-10: Civil Affairs Operations*. Washington, DC: GPO, 1985.

---. *Field Manual 41-10: Civil Affairs Operations*. Washington, DC: GPO, 1993.

---. *Field Manual 41-10: Civil Affairs Operations*. Washington, DC: GPO, 2000.

Dionne, E.J., Jr. "The Obama Doctrine in Action." *Washington Post* (April 16, 2009). http://www.washington post.com/wp-dyn/content/article/2009/04/5/AR2009041502902.html (accessed Mar 22, 2010).

Duff, Murray J. "Civil Affairs Force Structure: Is It Sufficient to Support Divisions and Corps in Contingency Operations?" Fort Leavenworth, KS: US Army Command and General Staff College, 1996. http://cgsc.cdmhost.com/cdm4/item_viewer.php?CISOROOT=/ p4013coll3&CISOPTR=939.

Feikert, Andrew. "U.S. Special Operations Forces (SOF): Background and Issues for Congress." Washington, D.C.: Congressional Research Service, Library of Congress, 2006.

Fund for Peace. "FAQ & Methodology." *Foreign Policy.* http://www.foreignpolicy.com/articles/ 2009/06/22/2009_failed_states_index_faq_methodology (accessed Jan 26, 2010).

---. *Foreign Policy.* http://www.foreignpolicy.com/images/ 090624_2009_final_data.pdf (accessed Jan 26, 2010).

---. http://www.foreignpolicy.com/images/090624_2009_final_data.pdf. (accessed January 26, 2010).

---. "The Index of Failed States." *Foreign Policy.* http://www.foreignpolicy.com/ articles/2009/06/22/2009_failed_states_index_interactive_map_and_rankings. (accessed Jan 26, 2010).

Ghani, Ashraf and Clare Lockhart. *Fixing Failed States*. New York: Oxford University Press, 2008.

Global Security. "350th Civil Affairs Command," under "Military," http://www.globalsecurity.org/ military/agency/army/350ca-cmd.htm (accessed 21Mar10).

Gray, Colin. War, Peace, and International Relations: An Introduction to Strategic History. New York: Routledge, 2007.

Grimes, Gregory. "Civil Affairs: Gathering the Reigns." *Small Wars Journal.* www.smallwarsjournal.com.

Hartzel, Thomas. Briefing. "CA Force Structure Analysis." Fort Bragg, N.C: USASOC, 2008.

---. Briefing. "TAA 10-15 CA and PSYOP Approved Growth." Fort Bragg, NC: USASOC, 2008.

Hicks, Kathleen H. and Cristine E. Wormuth. "The Future of U.S. Civil Affairs: A Report of the CSIS International Security Program." Washington, D.C.: Center for Strategic and International Studies, 2009.

Joint Staff. Joint Pub 3-07: *Doctrine for Joint Operations in Low Intensity Conflict*. Washington, DC: Joint Staff, 1990.

Joint Chiefs of Staff. Joint Publication 3-07: Joint Doctrine for Military Operations Other Than War. Washington, D.C.: Joint Staff, 1995.

---. *Joint Publication 3-57: Joint Doctrine for Civil Military Operations*. Washington, DC: Joint Staff, 1991.

---. Joint Publication 3-57: *Joint Doctrine for Civil Military Operations*. Washington, DC: Joint Staff, 1995.

---. Joint Publication 3-57: *Joint Doctrine for Civil Military Operations*. Washington, DC: Joint Staff, 2001.

---. Joint Publication 3-57: *Joint Doctrine for Civil Military Operations*. Washington, DC: Joint Staff, 2003.

---. *National Military Strategy of the United States*. Washington, DC: Joint Staff, 1992.

---. *National Military Strategy of the United States of America 1995: A Strategy of Flexible and Selective Engagement*. Washington, DC: Joint Chiefs of Staff, 1995. http://purl.access.gpo.gov/GPO/LPS24434.

---. *National military strategy: Shape, Respond, Prepare Now: A Military Strategy for a New Era*. Washington, DC: Joint Chiefs of Staff, 1997. http://purl.access.gpo.gov/GPO/LPS49289.

---. *The National Military Strategy of the United States of America: A Strategy for Today, a Vision for Tomorrow*. Washington, DC: Joint Chiefs of Staff, 2004. http://purl.access.gpo.gov/GPO/LPS59035.

Kimmey, Mark L. "Transforming Civil Affairs." *Army* 55 (Mar 2005).

Kitson, Frank. *Low Intensity Operations: Subversion, Insurgency, and Peacekeeping*. St. Petersburg, FL: Hailer.

Klinger, Janeen M. "International Relations Theory and American Grand Strategy." *U.S. Army War College Guide to National Security Issues*. Vol 2. 3 ed. Ed. J. Boone Bartholomees, Jr. Carlisle, PA: United States Army War College, 2008.

Kolb, Lawrence J. "Fixing the Mix." *Foreign Affairs* 83, no. 2 (March 2004).

Kusumoto, Dominic, "What should USSOCOM's Active Duty Civil Affairs Force Structure Look Like in the 21st Century?" (Maxwell Air Force Base, AL: Air Command and Staff College, 2008), 1-2.

Layne, Christopher. The Peace of Illusions: American Grand Strategy from 1940 to the Present. Ithaca, NY: Cornell University Press, 2006.

Maoz, Zeev and Azar Gat. *War in a Changing World*. Ann Arbor: University of Michigan Press, 2001.

Martin, Darrell W. "Restructuring of the United States Army Civil Affairs." Fort Leavenworth, KS: U.S. Army Command and General Staff College, 2004. http://cgsc.cdmhost.com/cdm4/item_viewer.php?CISOROOT=/p4013coll2&CISOPTR=222.

Martinage, Robert. "Special Operations Forces: Future Challenges and Opportunities." Washington, D.C.: Center for Strategic and Budgetary Assessments, 2008.

Marshall, Monty G. and Benjamin R. Cole. "Global Report on Conflict, Governance, and State Fragility 2008." *Foreign Policy Bulletin* (Winter 2008). http://www.systemicpeace.org/Global%20Report%202008.pdf accessed Jan 23, 2010.

McDougall, Walter A. *Promised Land, Crusader State: The American Encounter with the World Since 1776*. New York: Houghton Mifflin, 1997.

Mead, Walter Russell. *Special Providence: American Foreign Policy and How It Changed the World*. New York: Routledge, 2002.

Meinhart, Richard M. "National Military Strategies: 1990 to 2007." In U.S. Army War College Guide to National Security Issues. Vol 2. 3rd ed. Ed. J. Boone Bartholomees, Jr. Carlisle, PA: United States Army War College, 2008.

Naylor, Sean D. "Demand Skyrocketing for Active-Duty Civil Affairs Brigade." Oct 5, 2009. http://www.defensenews.com/osd_story.php?sh=VSDA&i=3755343. Accessed Nov 20, 2009.

Nere, Richard. "Democracy Promotion and the U.S. National Security Strategy: U.S. National Interest, U.S. Primacy, and Coercion." *Strategic Insights*. 8, no. 3 (August 2009). http://www.nps.edu/Academics/centers/ ccc/publications/OnlineJournal/2009/Aug/nereAug09.pdf (accessed Dec 1, 2009).

Nye, Joseph S., Jr. *Soft Power: The Means to Success in World Politics*. New York: Public Affairs, 2004.

Pillar, Paul R. *Terrorism and U.S. Foreign Policy*. Washington, D.C.: Brookings Institute Press, 2003.

Priniotakis, Manolis and Judith Miller. *Countering Insurgency and Promoting Democracy*. New York: Council for Emerging National Security Affairs, 2007.

Reimer, Jordan. "Review Drops Two-War Force Size Paradigm." American Forces Press Service (March 10, 2010). http://www.defense.gov/news/newsarticle.aspx?id=58273 (accessed March 27, 2010).

Rice, Susan E. and Stewart Patrick. *Index of State Weakness in the Developing World*, (Washington, D.C.: The Brookings Institution, 2008

Russett, Bruce. *Grasping the Democratic Peace*. New Jersey: Princeton University Press, 1993.

Sandler, Stanley. Glad to See Them Come and Sorry to See Them Go: A History of U.S. Army Civil Affairs and Military Government. Washington, D.C.: G.P.O., 2004.

U.S. President. *A National Security Strategy for a Global Age*. Washington, DC: GPO, 2000.

---. *A National Security Strategy for a New Century.* Washington, DC: GPO, 1999. http://purl.access.gpo.gov/GPO/LPS21835

---. *A National Security Strategy of Engagement and Enlargement.* Washington, DC: GPO, 1995. http://purl.access.gpo.gov/GPO/LPS48899.

---. Address. "Remarks by the President in Address to the Nation on the Way Forward in Afghanistan and Pakistan." http://www.whitehouse.gov/the-press-office/remarks-president-address-nation-way-forward-afghanistan-and-pakistan (accessed Mar 23, 2010).

---. *The National Security Strategy of the United States.* Washington, DC: GPO, 1991.

---. *The National Security Strategy of the United States.* Washington, DC: GPO, 1997. http://purl.access.gpo.gov/GPO/LPS21835.

---. *The National Security Strategy of the United States.* Washington, DC: GPO, 2002. http://purl.access.gpo.gov/GPO/LPS90878

---. *The National Security Strategy of the United States.* Washington, DC: GPO, 2006. http://purl.access.gpo.gov/GPO/LPS67777

U.S. Secretary of Defense. Speech to the Association of the United States Army. Washington, D.C., October 5, 2009. http://www.defense.gov/speeches/speech.aspx?speechid=1357 (accessed March 23, 2010).

---. Speech to the International Institute for Strategic Studies, Singapore, Indonesia, May 30, 2009. http://www.defense.gov/speeches/speech.aspx?speechid=1383, (accessed March 23, 2010).

U.S. Secretary of State. "Statement before the Senate Foreign Relations Committee." Nomination Hearing, January 13, 2009. http://www.state.gov/secretary/rm/2009a/01/115196.htm (accessed March 22, 2010).

U.S. Special Operations Command. *Fact Book: United States Special Operations Command.* Tampa, FL: USSOCOM, 2010. http://www.socom.mil/SOCOMHome/newspub/pubs/Documents/FactBook.pdf (accessed 22Mar10).

VanRoosen, Hugh C. "Implications of the 2006 Reassignment of U.S. Army Civil Affairs." Carlisle Barracks, PA: U.S. Army War College, 2009.